The **Guardian**
stylebook

The **Guardian**
stylebook

David Marsh and Nikki Marshall

First published in 2004 by Guardian Books
Guardian Books in an imprint of Guardian Newspapers Ltd

Copyright © Guardian Newspapers Ltd 2004

The Guardian is a registered trademark of the
Guardian Media Groups Plc and Guardian Newspapers Ltd

A CIP record for this book is available from the
British Library

ISBN 1 84354 991 3

Distributed by Atlantic Books,
an imprint of Grove Atlantic Ltd, Ormond House,
26-27 Boswell Street, London WC1N 3JZ

Printed in Great Britain by Cambridge University Press

Cover Design: Two Associates
Text Design: www.carrstudio.co.uk

Contents

Acknowledgments

Special thanks to Richard Alcock, John Ardill, Andy Bodle, Andrew Dilnott, Julie Harris, Amelia Hodsdon, Farhana Hoque, Barry Johnson, Chris Mackay, Dominic Marsh, Tom Murphy, Paul Olive, Tim Radford, Ben Summers, Ali Usman, Brian Whitaker, and in particular Hannah Forbes Black.

Thanks also to all the many Guardian staff and readers who have contributed ideas, suggestions, angry protests and bitter complaints: we appreciate them all

Dedication

In loving memory of Patrick Rupert David Marsh (1979-2003), who was the first person to point out the crucial distinction between WWE and WWF

Preface: Moments of revelation

Ian Mayes

Several hundred journalists contribute to any day's edition of the Guardian, and they make mistakes. Some people like this fallibility in their paper, or at least they tolerate it amiably. They refer endearingly to the result of all the sweat, blood and tears as the Grauniad. They find the occasional blemish a welcome reassurance that a human hand is still at work behind the increasing layers of sophisticated technology. It is well to keep a sense of proportion. As the Spanish proverb says: he is always right who suspects that he is always making mistakes.

This is the first Guardian style guide to be made generally available as a book and it offers plenty of evidence that the tendency to err is not accepted complacently. When you scream or tear your hair, be assured that similar cries of anguish, frustration or rage are ringing in Farringdon Road. Particular wrath is visited upon repeat offenders. Under "biblical references", for example, a reminder that the Apocalypse is the book of Revelation and not Revelations is accompanied by the blood-curdling promise: "Anyone calling it 'Revelations' will burn in hell for eternity" – a touching acknowledgment of an afterlife, perhaps not shared by EE Cummings. He wrote: "… for life's not a paragraph/ And death i think is no parenthesis." See the entry for Cummings (capital initials for his name despite the preference for lower case in his poetry); and for "parenthesis" look under "brackets". Do not neglect to turn to "capitals" for an exposition of the most contentious style issue in the Guardian in recent years. Initially (not wishing to pun) the changes gave some readers the impression that the paper was composed in "a whimsical medley of lower case and capital letters", a phrase used by the novelist Clare Messud to describe the efforts of someone painstakingly learning English as a second language. All the comments were carefully listened to and some amendments introduced that have made the logic of the capitalisation policy more accessible and persuasive. It is one of many examples of responsiveness to readers that make the stylebook participatory.

Nothing escapes the attention of the Guardian's readers. There are many for whom our pursuit of precision is an agony, too vaguely and limply prosecuted. They constantly urge us on. Some persistent errors have almost been eradicated by repeatedly drawing attention to them publicly in the Guardian's daily corrections and clarifications column. Lucian Freud is now only rarely called Lucien. Johns Hopkins University in Baltimore is less frequently called John Hopkins. Colombia, the country in South America, makes fewer appearances as Columbia, as in District of Columbia. Middlesbrough should before long stand its rightful ground against the interloper Middlesborough, which still keeps it under siege (not seige). Employment tribunals, years after the name was introduced, may soon succeed in displacing the redundant industrial tribunals.

A newspaper, because of the volume of its contents and the speed with which it is assembled, might be called an engine for making mistakes. It might also, just as legitimately, be said to spread before us a battlefield on which may be observed all the present conflicts in the English language, in particular the struggle between conservative and progressive tendencies. The tolerance, within certain boundaries, of swearwords that remain taboo in most other newspapers is an acknowledgment of their prevalence in society. The Guardian's guidelines would, perhaps, be more generally seen as sensible if they were adhered to. It may be that one distant day we have to concede "like" as an alternative to "such as", or "enormity" for "enormous", or "refute" for "rebut", or "fulsome" for "wholehearted", but, happily, not yet. We might almost risk saying there will never be any concession on flaunt for flout, mitigate for militate, the frequent reversal of underestimate and overestimate, or procrastinate for the near libellous prevaricate, all of which are simply wrong.

Many of the entries are descriptive of the Guardian ethos: those that set out the rules for references to asylum seekers (there is no such thing as an illegal asylum seeker), or mental illness, or physical disability, or gender, for example. These things do matter. More people write to me, as readers' editor, about the Guardian's use, or misuse of English, than any other subject. The editors of the stylebook, David Marsh and Nikki Marshall, have laboured long and lovingly at their Sisyphean task. Will it have been worth it, after all? Undoubtedly, or as we have been known to say on occasion, undoubtably. Above all, it is a plea for consistency, or to get as close to it as is humanly possible.

Ian Mayes is the readers' editor of the Guardian

Introduction: Amok or amuck?

This is the sixth Guardian stylebook, but the first to be published for sale to the general public and not just for use by the paper's staff.

The first "Style-book of the Manchester Guardian", as it then was, appeared in November 1928 under the auspices of the great CP Scott, then well into his sixth decade as editor. (You can read his brilliant essay on the 100th anniversary of the paper in an appendix to this book.) A few entries have survived intact through the decades into this edition.

In addition to such vital information as what to call domestic servants — cook general (two words), housemaid (one word), kitchen-maid (hyphenated) — the first book reminded staff to capitalise CHANCELLOR of the EXCHEQUER, warned gravely that Sinn Féin were "Extreme Republicans", and advised: "When a compositor cannot decipher a word, it is better to put in a blank than a word that is obviously wrong."

That book lasted until 1960, when a new edition heralded the swinging 60s with the daring decision to drop the kitchenmaid's hyphen. The third edition, in 1969, was notable for this plea from the paper's then editor, Alastair Hetherington: "In news stories, would writers and subeditors please put the point at the beginning?"

The kitchenmaid survived that revision, but not the next, a decade later (by which time Yorkshire pudding had become yorkshire pudding). However, such Guardian eccentricities as "gaol" for jail were not abandoned until the late 80s and the fifth edition, a chaotic volume in which concern for mere words was all but lost amid pages of instruction on how to use the industry's then novel computer technology. (The confusion was typified by the rather wonderful "amok, rather than amuck"; followed, two entries later, by: "amuck, not amok".)

The style guide's first duty is to Guardian journalists, but when, in 2000, the computer system was upgraded to give us access to the world wide web we jumped at the chance to put it online. This was a first. It means Guardian house style can be updated and expanded as needed. As society changes so does the way we use language, and we like to be in the vanguard of this movement. From the moment we went online the style guide no longer existed in printed form.

The bonus was the dialogue this encouraged with readers. We have gone on to incorporate many of their suggestions and correct mistakes they've pointed out. And we get feedback from around the world from people thanking us for helping them to win an argument, or telling us they've adopted our house style for their business or publication. Emails range from the effusive — "The Guardian style guide is one of the best and linguistically most progressive I have seen. I can tell you it is widely used by members of English departments in many universities in Europe" — to the abusive: "The people of Madagascar do not call themselves Madagascans. Believe me. You are idiots."

Adding and editing entries can be incredibly time-consuming and journalists don't like it when we move the goalposts by changing the guide without notifying them. Generally we work towards two revisions a year, so we can announce changes together. We also maintain an electronic noticeboard to discuss style points and call interested parties together for lunchtime meetings to debate big changes and any points anyone wants to raise. But if there's an error that needs fixing or a new word in the news we can make changes straight away. The style guide covers all Guardian publications. That isn't to say these don't each have their own voice but our broad guidelines apply across the board.

The online style guide will continue, but there are two drawbacks: not everyone, yet, has access to the web; and, even among many who do, there is a desire for the printed word that electronic media fail to satisfy. So it is in response to requests from many readers — those who through the internet are already familiar with our style, and those who would like to be — that we return to the printed page.

Whether online or on paper, we want the words we use in the Guardian to work as hard as they can, which means the language we choose must be clean, contemporary and consistent. Inconsistency is distracting and gets in the way of what we're saying, and house style exists to help us communicate with readers. Many of these entries shape the language we use when dealing with, for example, race, gender, illness and disability, to reflect the paper's values and the point of view of the people we are writing about. The book also warns against common errors of grammar and fact. That said, the unthinking application of any style guide will create more errors than it avoids — these recommendations must always be applied with common sense, and (almost) all the rules may have to be broken at some time or other. If you can't find something you want in this book, follow Collins, our favourite dictionary.

A style guide should be much more than a list of words and grammatical rules. Such rules change, and some can be arbitrary or baseless. Jonathan Swift, who wanted to "ascertain" the language so that "our best Writings might be preserved with Care", was one in a long line who didn't get it. His heirs — those who complain about the way "gay" is now used, about denying the foreign secretary his capital letters ("how do we know you aren't talking about a French typist?"), about so-called split infinitives — don't get it either. Language changes. The trick is to reconcile this process with a set of guidelines that, while capable of acknowledging and responding to change, ensure that we use a word, or spell a name, the same way on page 91 of the magazine as on page 1 of the newspaper.

But there's more to it than that. We follow a style guide to be consistent and coherent, and to make fewer mistakes, but above all because the style of a newspaper should reflect what we stand for and the respect we accord those we write about. The words within may evolve, but the Guardian remains true to its values. CP Scott would expect nothing less.

David Marsh and **Nikki Marshall**
June 2004

The style guide is online at www.guardian.co.uk/styleguide
The email address for your comments, which we welcome, is
style.guide@guardian.co.uk

Glossary

adjectives modify nouns, as in "she had a quick drink"

adverbs modify verbs, as in "she drank quickly"

blurb copy pointing to an article elsewhere in the newspaper or one of its other publications

cap up start the word with a capital letter

captions text describing a photograph or image

City short for City of London, the capital's financial centre

compositor a person who set type for printing (before newspaper pages were created on computer programs)

copy the main body text of an article

desk editors journalists who plan their section's coverage and assign stories to reporters

display quotes extracts from an article reproduced in a larger type, set into the body of the text

editor is to newspaper as captain is to ship

Fleet Street nickname for Britain's national newspapers (their former home)

full out write in full

G2 the Guardian's features section

headline, head text in large bold type trumpeting an article

italicise use italics, like *this*

lc lower case

leader article in comment pages expressing the opinion of the Guardian

line break where a line of copy ends

reporters gather news and write articles for newspapers

roman ordinary lettering, not bold or italicised

running text the main body copy of an article

spike reject a story (named for the metal spike on which pages of unwanted copy were impaled)

sources people willing to talk to journalists

'Style to be good must be clear. Clearness is secured by using words that are current and ordinary'

Aristotle Rhetoric 3:2

spin usually refers to public relations strategies used by a government to cast a flattering light on its activities

standfirsts a sub-heading or secondary headline, in smaller text and often running across a page and above a photograph

story not a work of fiction, but a news article or feature

subeditor, sub journalist who lays out (designs) pages, edits, checks and cuts copy, and writes headlines, captions and standfirsts

tabloid refers to long-standing redtops such as the Sun and the Daily Mirror, rather than the new breed of shrunken broadsheets

tabloidese punning, sensational style beloved of tabloid journalists

thin (non-breaking) space inserted by subeditors between words that should not straddle a line break, eg 2 million

transitive verbs take an object, as in the sentence "she stroked the cat" **intransitive verbs** do not take an object, as in "his dog died"

transliteration writing one language in the alphabet of another

uc UPPER CASE

wires breaking stories and features written by staff at news agencies such as Reuters and sent by direct line to subscribing newspapers

a or an before h? use an only if the h is silent: an hour, an heir, an honourable man, an honest woman; but a hero, a hotel, a historian (but don't change a direct quote if the speaker says, for example, "an historic")

abattoir

abbeys cap up, eg Rievaulx Abbey, Westminster Abbey

abbreviations
Do not use full points in abbreviations, or spaces between initials: BBC, US, mph, eg, 4am, lbw, No 10, PJ O'Rourke, WH Smith, etc.
   Spell out less well-known abbreviations on first mention; it is not necessary to spell out well-known ones, such as EU, UN, US, BBC, CIA, FBI, CD, Aids, Nasa.
   Use all caps only if the abbreviation is pronounced as the individual letters; otherwise spell the word out: BBC, ICI, VAT, but Isa, Nato.

Beware of overusing less well-known acronyms and abbreviations; they can look clunky and clutter up text, especially those explained in brackets but then only referred to once or twice again. It is usually simpler to use another word, or even to write out the name in full a second time. *See contractions*

Aborigines, Aboriginal cap up when referring to native Australians

aborigines, aboriginal lc when referring to indigenous populations

abscess

absorption

abysmal

abyss

a cappella

Acas the Advisory, Conciliation and Arbitration Service at first mention, thereafter just Acas

accents use on French, German, Spanish and Irish Gaelic words (but not anglicised French words such as cafe, apart from exposé, resumé)

Accenture formerly Andersen Consulting

access has been known as **contact** since the 1989 Children Act

accommodate, accommodation

accordion

achilles heel, achilles tendon

acknowledgment not acknowledgement

acronyms take initial cap, eg Aids, Isa, Mori, Nato

act uc when using full name, eg Criminal Justice Act 1998, Official Secrets Act; but lc on second reference, eg "the act", and when speaking in more general terms, eg "we need a radical freedom of information act"; bills remain lc until passed into law

acting always lc: acting prime minister, acting committee chair, etc

actor male and female: avoid actress except when in name of award, eg Oscar for best actress. One 27-year-old actor contacted the Guardian to say "actress" has acquired a faintly pejorative tinge and she wants people to call her actor (except for her agent who should call her often)

AD, BC AD goes before the date (AD64), BC goes after (300BC); both go after the century, eg second century AD, fourth century BC

adaptation not adaption

addendum plural **addendums**

addresses 119 Farringdon Road, London EC1R 3ER

Adidas initial cap

administration the Clinton administration, etc

Adrenalin TM; a brand of adrenaline

adrenaline hormone that increases heart rate and blood pressure, extracted from animals or synthesised for medical uses

adverbs do not use hyphens
after adverbs ending in -ly,
eg a hotly disputed penalty, a
constantly evolving newspaper,
genetically modified food, etc;
but hyphens are needed with
short and common adverbs,
eg an ill prepared report,
a hard-bitten hack

adviser not advisor

advocate member of the
Scottish bar (not a barrister)

aeroplane not airplane

affect/effect exhortations in
the style guide had no effect
(noun) on the number of
mistakes; the level of mistakes
was not affected (verb) by
exhortations in the style guide;
we hope to effect (verb) a
change in this

affinity with or between, not to
or for

Afghans people
Afghanis currency of Afghanistan

aficionado
plural **aficionados**

African-Caribbean not
Afro-Caribbean

Afrikaans language
Afrikaner person

ageing

ages Tony Blair, 51 (not
"aged 51"); little Johnny, four;
the woman was in her 20s
(but twentysomething,
fortysomething)

aggravate to make worse,
not to annoy

aggro despite the once
popular terrace chant
"A, G, A-G-R, A-G-R-O: Agro!"

AGM

ahead of avoid, use before or
in advance of

aide-de-camp
plural **aides-de-camp**

aide-memoire
plural **aide-memoires**

Aids acquired immune
deficiency syndrome, but
normally no need to spell out

**airbase, aircrew, airdrop,
airlift, airmail**

aircraft carrier

air raid, air strike

air vice-marshal

al- (note lc and hyphen) before an Arabic name means "the" so try to avoid writing "the al- ... " where possible

Alastair or Alistair?
Alastair Campbell,
Alastair Hetherington
Alistair Cooke, Alistair Darling,
Alistair Maclean, Alistair McGowan
Aleister Crowley

Albright, Madeleine former US secretary of state; Mrs Albright, not Ms, after first mention

Alcott, Louisa May (1832-88) American author of Little Women

A-levels

Ali, Muhammad

alibi being somewhere else; not synonymous with excuse

alice band as worn by Alice in the original illustrations to Lewis Carroll's Through the Looking-Glass (1871) and David Beckham

Allah Arabic for "the God". Both words refer to the same concept: there is no major difference between God in the Old Testament and Allah in Islam. Therefore it makes sense to talk about "God" in an Islamic context and to use "Allah" in quotations or for literary effect

Allahu Akbar "God is most great"

all comers

Allende, Isabel Chilean author, niece of Salvador

Allende, Salvador Chilean president, overthrown and killed in 1973

allies lc, second world war allies, etc; but use coalition when referring to the 2003 Iraq war

all mouth and trousers not "all mouth and no trousers", as has appeared in the paper

allot, allotted

all right is right; alright is not all right

All Souls College, Oxford no apostrophe

Almodóvar, Pedro Spanish film-maker

alsatian dog

AltaVista

alternative strictly, a choice between two courses of action;

if there are more than two, option or choice may be preferred

alumnus plural **alumni**

Alzheimer's disease

AM (assembly member) member of the Welsh assembly, eg Rhodri Morgan AM

ambassador lc, eg the British ambassador to Washington

American Civil Liberties Union not American Civil Rights Union

American universities Take care: "University of X" is not the same as "X University"; most states have two large public universities, eg University of Kentucky and Kentucky State University, University of Illinois and Illinois State University, etc.
   Do not call Johns Hopkins University "John Hopkins" or Stanford University "Stamford"

America's Cup

Amhrán na bhFiann Irish national anthem

Amicus trade union formed by a merger between the AEEU and MSF

amid not amidst

amok not amuck

among not amongst

among or between? Contrary to popular myth, between is not limited to two parties. It is appropriate when the relationship is essentially reciprocal: fighting between the many peoples of Yugoslavia, treaties between European countries. Among belongs to distributive relationships: shared among, etc

ampersand use in company names when the company does: Marks & Spencer, P&O

anaesthetic

analysis plural **analyses**

ancestors precede descendants; we frequently manage to get them the wrong way round

Andalucía

annex verb **annexe** noun

anonymous pejorative quotes See appendix 2: the editor's guidelines on the identification of sources

Ansaphone TM; use answering machine or answerphone

antenna, antennae, antennas antenna (insect), plural antennae; antenna (radio), plural antennas

anticipate take action in expectation of; not synonymous with expect

anticlimax

antidepressants

antihero

antipodes

anti-semitic, anti-war but **antisocial**

any more two words

apex plural apexes

apostrophes
Some plural nouns have no "s", eg children. These take an apostrophe and "s" in the possessive, eg children's games, gentlemen's outfitter, old folk's home.

The possessive in words and names ending in s normally takes an apostrophe followed by a second s (Jones's, James's), but be guided by pronunciation and use the plural apostrophe where

it helps: Mephistopheles' rather than Mephistopheles's.

Use apostrophes in phrases such as in two days' time, 12 years' imprisonment and six weeks' holiday, where the time period (two days) modifies a noun (time), but not in nine months pregnant or three weeks old, where the time period is adverbial (modifying an adjective such as pregnant or old) — if in doubt, test with a singular such as one day's time, one month pregnant.

And if anyone tries to tell you that apostrophes don't matter and we'd be better off without them, consider these four phrases (listed in Steven Pinker's The Language Instinct), each of which means something completely different:
my sister's friend's investments,
my sisters' friends' investments,
my sisters' friend's investments,
my sister's friends' investments

appal, appalling

appendix plural **appendices**

appraise to estimate worth

apprise to inform

aquarium plural **aquariums**

Arab

Both a noun and an adjective, and the preferred adjective when referring to Arab things in general, eg Arab history, Arab traditions. Arabic usually refers to the language and literature: "the Arabic press" means newspapers written in Arabic, while "the Arab press" would include newspapers produced by Arabs in other languages.

There is no simple definition of an Arab. At an international level, the 22 members of the Arab League can safely be described as Arab countries: Algeria, Bahrain, Comoros, Djibouti, Egypt, Iraq, Jordan, Kuwait, Lebanon, Libya, Mauritania, Morocco, Oman, Palestine, Qatar, Saudi Arabia, Somalia, Sudan, Syria, Tunisia, United Arab Emirates and Yemen. At a human level, there are substantial groups within those countries — the Berbers of north Africa and the Kurds, for example — who do not regard themselves as Arabs.

Arabic

Though Arabic has only three vowels — a, i and u — it has several consonants that have no equivalent in the Roman alphabet. For instance, there are two kinds of s, d and t. There are also two kinds of glottal sound. This means there are at least 32 ways of writing the Libyan leader Muammar Gadafy's name in English, and a reasonable argument can be made for adopting almost any of them. With no standard approach to transliteration agreed by the western media, we must try to balance consistency, comprehensibility and familiarity – which often puts a strain on all three.

Typically, Arabs have at least three names. In some cases the first or second name may be the one that is most used, and this does not imply familiarity (Arabs often address foreigners politely as "Mr John" or "Dr David"). Saddam, for example, is used by western and Arab media alike because it is more unusual than Hussein. And often Arabs also have familiar names that have no connection with the names on their identity cards; a man might become known after the birth of his first son as "Abu Ahmad", the father of Ahmad (eg the Palestinian leader Ahmed Qureia is commonly known as Abu Ala).

'Iraq or Iran – what's our style?'

Freelance subeditor
at British national newspaper
(not the Guardian)

Where a particular spelling has become widely accepted through usage we should retain it. Where an individual with links to the west has clearly adopted a particular spelling of his or her own name, we should respect that. For breaking news and stories using names for which the Guardian has no established style, we take the lead given by Reuters wire copy.

Note also that names in some parts of the Arab world have become gallicised, while others have become anglicised, eg the leading Egyptian film director Youssef Chahine uses a French spelling instead of the English transliteration, Shaheen.

Some guidelines (for use particularly where there is no established transliteration):
al-
Means "the". In names it is not capitalised, eg Ahmad al-Saqqaf, and can be dropped after the first mention (Mr Saqqaf). For placenames the Guardian drops it altogether. Sometimes it appears as as- or ash- or ad- or ul-: these should be ignored and can be safely rewritten as al-. But some Arabs, including Syrians and Egyptians, prefer to use el- in place of al-.

Exceptions: by convention, **Allah** (al-Lah, literally "the God") is written as one word and capitalised; and in Saudi royal names, **Al Saud** is correct (in this case, "al" is actually "aal" and does not mean "the").

abdul, abu and **bin**
These are not self-contained names, but are connected to the name that follows: **abdul** means "slave of … " and so cannot correctly be used on its own. There are standard combinations, "slave of the merciful one", "slave of the generous one", etc, which all indicate that the person is a servant of God. In transliteration, "abd" (slave) is lower case, eg Ahmad abd al-Rahman al-Saqqaf, except when used at the start of a name.

abu (father of) and **bin** (son of) are similar. When they appear in the middle of a name they should be lower case and are used in combination with the following part of the name: Faisal abu Ahmad al-Saqqaf, Faisal bin Ahmad al-Saqqaf.

Despite the above, some people are actually known as "Abdul". This is more common among non-Arab Muslims. And some Arabs run "abd" or "abu" into the following word, eg the writer Abdelrahman Munif.

Muhammad
Our style for the prophet's name and for most Muhammads living in Arab countries, though where someone's preferred spelling is known we respect it, eg Mohamed Al Fayed, Mohamed ElBaradei. The spelling Mohammed (or variants) is considered archaic by most British Muslims, and disrespectful by many of them.

Muhandis/Mohandes, Qadi
Be wary of names where the first word is Muhandis or Qadi: these are honorary titles, meaning engineer and judge respectively

Arafat, Yasser

archbishops the Archbishop of Canterbury, (the Most Rev) Rowan Williams, at first mention, thereafter Dr Williams or the archbishop; the Archbishop of Westminster, Cardinal Cormac Murphy-O'Connor, on first mention, subsequently Cardinal Murphy-O'Connor or the archbishop

archdeacon the Ven Paul Olive, Archdeacon of Farringdon, at first mention; then Mr Olive (unless he is a Dr), or the archdeacon

archipelago
plural **archipelagos**

Ardoyne (Belfast), not "the Ardoyne"

Argentinian noun and adjective

arguably unarguably one of the most overused words in the language

armed forces, armed services
the army, the **British army**, **the navy**, but **Royal Navy**, **Royal Air Force** (RAF is OK)

arms akimbo hands on hips, elbows out; we have had "legs akimbo" in the paper (uncomfortable as well as ungrammatical)

around about or approximately are better, eg "about £1m" or "approximately 2,000 people"

arranged marriages are a traditional and perfectly acceptable form of wedlock across southern Asia and within the Asian community in Britain;

they should not be confused with **forced marriages**, which are arranged without the consent of one or both partners, and have been widely criticised

artist not artiste (except, possibly, in a historical context)

art movements lc, **art deco, art nouveau, cubism, dadaism, gothic, impressionism, pop art, surrealism**, etc, but **Bauhaus, Modern** (in the sense of Modern British, to distinguish it from "modern art"), **pre-Raphaelite, Romantic** (to differentiate between a romantic painting and a Romantic painting)

Arts Council

ascendancy, ascendant

Ashura a day of voluntary fasting for Muslims; Shia Muslims also commemorate the martyrdom of Hussein, a grandson of the prophet. For their community, therefore, it is not a festival but a day of deep mourning

aspirin

astrologer not astrologist

Asunción capital of Paraguay

asylum seeker
Someone seeking refugee status or humanitarian protection; there is no such thing as a "bogus" or "illegal" asylum seeker. Refugees are people who have fled their home countries in fear for their lives, and may have been granted asylum under the 1951 refugee convention or qualify for humanitarian protection or discretionary leave, or have been granted exceptional leave to remain in Britain. An asylum seeker can only become an illegal immigrant if he or she remains in Britain after having failed to respond to a removal notice

athletics 1500m but **5,000m** (the former is the "fifteen hundred" not "one thousand five hundred" metres)

Atlantic Ocean or just the Atlantic

attache no accent

Attlee, Clement (1883-1967) Labour prime minister 1945-51, often misspelt as Atlee

attorney general lc, no hyphen

auger used to make holes
augur predict or presage

Aum Shinrikyo means Supreme Truth sect, but note that the "aum" means sect, so to talk about the "Aum sect" or "Aum cult" is tautologous

au pair

Australian Labor party not Labour

autism an incurable neurological disorder, to be used only when referring to the condition, not as a term of abuse, or in producing such witticisms as "mindless moral autism" and "Star Wars is a form of male autism", both of which have appeared in the paper; autistic means someone with autism, not someone with poor social skills

Autocue TM; **teleprompter** is a generic alternative

avant garde no hyphen

awards, prizes, medals generally lc, eg Guardian first book award, Nobel peace prize, Fields medal (exceptions: the Academy Awards, Victoria Cross); note that categories are lc, eg "he took the best actor Oscar at the awards"

axis plural **axes**

Azerbaijan noun **Azerbaijani** adjective; note that there are ethnic **Azeris** living in, for example, Armenia

Aziz, Tariq former deputy prime minister of Iraq

Aznar, José María former prime minister of Spain

BAA do not call it the British Airports Authority, its former name

Ba'ath

Babybel cheese

baby Bells US regional telephone companies formed after the breakup of AT&T in 1984

backbench newspaper or politics; **backbenches, backbenchers**

backstreet

bacteria plural of **bacterium**, so don't write "the bacteria is"

BAE Systems formerly British Aerospace

Baghdad

bail out a prisoner, a company or person in financial difficulty; the noun is **bail-out**; but **bale out** a boat or from an aircraft

bakewell tart

balk obstruct, pull up, stop short; **baulk** area of a snooker table

ballot, balloted

Band-Aid TM; say **plaster** or **sticking plaster**

band names lc the: the Beatles, the Black Eyed Peas, the The; but uc equivalents in other languages, eg Les Négresses Vertes, Los Lobos

Bank of England the Bank (uc) is acceptable on subsequent mentions

bank holiday

banknote

bar (legal) she was called to the bar; (political) of the House of Commons

barbecue

Barclays Bank

barcode

barmitzvah, batmitzvah

Barnardo's children's charity, formerly Dr Barnardo's; it no longer runs orphanages

barolo wine

barons, baronesses we call them lords and ladies, even at first mention: Lady Thatcher, Lady Blackstone, Lady Jay, Lord Callaghan, etc

Barons Court

baroque

Basle not Basel

Basque country

bas-relief

Battenberg (not Battenburg) German family name that became Mountbatten; **battenberg cake** lc

battlebus

Bauhaus

B&B abbreviation for bed and breakfast

BBC1, BBC2, BBC3, BBC4
no spaces

1000BC but **AD1066**
See AD

B&Q

beau plural **beaux**

bebop, hard bop, post-bop

Becket, Thomas (1118-70) murdered Archbishop of Canterbury, not Thomas à Becket

bed blocking

bedouin

beef wellington

Beeton, Mrs (Isabella Mary Beeton, 1836-65) author of the Book of Household Management

befitted

begs the question
A tricky one, best avoided since it is almost invariably misused: it means assuming a proposition that, in reality, involves the conclusion. An example would be to say that parallel lines will never meet because they are parallel, assuming as a fact the thing you are professing to prove. What it does not mean is "raises the question"

Beijing

Belarus
adjective **Belarussian**

believable

Bell's whisky

bellwether sheep that leads
the herd; customarily misspelt,
misused, or both

benefited, benefiting

Benetton

Berchtesgaden

berks and wankers
Kingsley Amis identified two
principal groups in debates over
use of language: "Berks are
careless, coarse, crass, gross
and of what anybody would
agree is a lower social class than
one's own; wankers are prissy,
fussy, priggish, prim and of
what they would probably
misrepresent as a higher social
class than one's own"

Bernabéu stadium Madrid

Betaferon TM; the generic
term for the drug is
interferon-beta 1b

bete noire no accent

betting odds
These are meaningless to
many readers, and we frequently
get them wrong. But here's a
brief explanation: Long odds
(eg 100-1 against, normally
expressed as 100-1) mean
something unlikely; shorter
odds (eg 10-1) still mean it's
unlikely, but less unlikely; odds
on (eg 2-1 on, sometimes
expressed as 1-2) means it is
likely, so if you were betting £2
you would win only £1 plus the
stake.

Take care using the phrase
"odds on": if Labour is quoted
by bookmakers at 3-1 to win a
byelection, and the odds are cut
to 2-1, it is wrong to say "the
odds on Labour to win were cut
last night" — in fact, the odds
against Labour to win have
been cut (the shorter the price,
the more likely something is
expected to happen).

It gets more complicated when
something is genuinely odds on,
ie bookmakers quote a price of
"2-1 on": in this case, if the
Labour candidate is quoted at
2-1 on and becomes an even
hotter favourite, at 3-1 on, the
odds have shortened; if Labour
loses popularity, and 2-1 on
becomes, say, 7-4 on or evens,
the odds have lengthened

Bevan, Aneurin Labour health minister (1945-51) and architect of the NHS, also known as Nye Bevan
Bevin, Ernest Labour foreign secretary (1945-51) who helped to create Nato

Beverly Hills

Beyoncé

biannual twice a year, **biennial** every two years; biannual is almost always misused: to avoid confusion stick with the alternative twice-yearly; two-yearly is an alternative to biennial

bias, biased

Bible cap up if referring to Old or New Testament; lc in such sentences as "the Guardian style guide is my bible"; **biblical** lc

biblical quotations
Use a modern translation, not the Authorised Version. From a reader: "Peradventure the editor hath no copy of Holy Writ in the office, save the King James Version only. Howbeit the great multitude of believers knoweth this translation not. And he (or she) who quoteth the words of Jesus in ancient form, sheweth plainly that he (or she) considereth them to be out of date. Wherefore let them be quoted in such manner that the people may understand"

biblical references Genesis 1:1; II Corinthians 2:13; Revelation 3:16 (anyone calling it "Revelations" will burn in hell for eternity)

bicentenary a 200th anniversary; **bicentennial** its adjective

biceps singular and plural, there is no such thing as a bicep

bid use only in a financial sense, eg Manchester United have made a bid for Henry, or for auctions

big usually preferable to major, massive, giant, mammoth, behemoth, etc, particularly in news copy

bigot, bigoted

bill lc, even when giving full name; cap up only if it becomes an act

billion one thousand million, not one million million: in copy use **bn** for sums of money, quantities or inanimate objects: £10bn, 1bn litres of water; otherwise billion: 6 billion people, etc; use bn in headlines

Birds Eye TM; no apostrophe

birdwatchers also known as **birders**, not "twitchers"; they go birdwatching or birding, not "twitching"

Biro TM; say **ballpoint pen**

birthplace, birthrate, birthright

Birtwistle, Sir Harrison British composer

bishops the Right Rev Clifford Richard, Bishop of Wimbledon, at first mention; thereafter the bishop or Bishop Richard; it is OK to leave out the Right Rev

bismillah means "in the name of God" in Arabic

black lc noun and adjective when referring to race

Black Country

black economy prefer hidden or parallel economy

black-on-black violence is banned, unless in a quote, but even then treat with scepticism (imagine the police saying they were "investigating an incident of white-on-white violence between Millwall and West Ham supporters")

blackout

Blair/Booth, Cherie wishes to be called **Mrs Blair** when we are referring to her role as the wife of the prime minister; if she is appearing in court or at a function related to her work as a lawyer, she is **Cherie Booth QC** (Ms Booth on second mention)

blase no accent

blastfurnace

bleeper not beeper; synonym for pager

blitz, blitzkrieg

blond adjective and male noun; **blonde** female noun: the woman is a blonde, because she has blond hair; the man has blond hair and is, if you insist, a blond

Bloody Sunday take care when writing about the death toll: 13 died in Derry on January 30 1972, but a 14th victim died from a brain tumour several months later, so we should use a phrase such as "which led to 14 deaths"

Bluffer's Guide TM; beware of using phrases like "a bluffer's guide to crimewriting", a headline that led to a complaint from the copyright holder

Blu-Tack TM

Boat Race Oxford v Cambridge

Boddingtons

bogey golf, ghost
bogie trolley, truck

Bogotá capital of Colombia

bogus take care: there is no such thing as a "bogus asylum seeker". *See asylum seeker*

Bombay *see Mumbai*

bona fide, bona fides

Bonham Carter, Helena

bookcase, bookkeeper, bookseller, bookshelf

book titles are not italicised, except in the newspaper's Review section; lc for a, an, and, of, on, the (unless they are the first word of the title): A Tale of Two Cities, The Pride and the Passion, etc

bon vivant not bon viveur

bordeaux wine

bored with, by not bored of

Boston Strangler

both unnecessary in most sentences that contain "and"; "both men and women" says no more than "men and women", and takes longer; if you do use it, it is plural: "both women have reached the tops of their professions"

bottleneck

Boudicca not Boadicea

Boundary Commission

bourgeois adjective
bourgeoisie noun

Boutros Boutros-Ghali former UN secretary general; Mr Boutros-Ghali at second mention

bovine somatotrophin (BST)

box office

boy male under 18

boyfriend

boy's own

brackets
If the sentence is logically and grammatically complete without the information contained within the parentheses (round brackets), the punctuation stays outside the brackets. (A complete sentence that stands alone in parentheses starts with a capital letter and ends with a stop.)

"Square brackets," the grammarian said, "are used in direct quotes when an interpolation [a note from the writer, not uttered by the speaker] is added to provide essential information."

braille

brand avoid tabloidese such as "Howard brands Blair a liar"

Brands Hatch no apostrophe

Brasilia capital of Brazil

breastfed, breastfeeding

'Journalism:
a profession whose business it is to explain to others what it personally does not understand'

Lord Northcliffe

briar bush, pipe

bric-a-brac

brickbat cliche, do not use

Bridgnorth

Brink's-Mat

Britain, UK
These terms are synonymous: Britain is the official short form of United Kingdom of Great Britain and Northern Ireland. Used as adjectives, therefore, British and UK mean the same. Great Britain, however, refers only to England, Wales and Scotland.

Take care not to write Britain when you might mean only England and Wales, for example when referring to the education system. *See Scotland*

Britart

British Council

British Film Institute BFI on second mention

British Library

British Medical Association (doctors' trade union), BMA on second mention

British Museum

Britpop

Britvic TM

brownie points

Brueghel family of Flemish painters

Brum, Brummie

brussels sprouts

brutalise render brutal, not treat brutally; so soldiers may be brutalised by the experience of war

Brylcreem TM

BSE bovine spongiform encephalopathy; no need to spell out

BST British summer time

Buckingham Palace the palace on second mention

buckminsterfullerene a form of carbon, named after the US engineer Buckminster Fuller (1895-1983)

budget, the lc noun and adjective, eg budget talks, budget measures, mini-budget, pre-budget report, etc

buffaloes not buffalos

Bulger, James not Jamie

Buñuel, Luis (1900-83) Spanish film director

Burberry TM

bureau plural **bureaus** (furniture) or **bureaux** (organisations)

burgomaster not burgomeister

burka not burqa

Burma not Myanmar

burned/burnt burned is the past tense form (he burned the cakes); burnt is the participle, an "adjectival" form of the verb (the cakes are burnt)

buses, bussed, bussing

Bush, George not George W; his father is George Bush Sr

businesslike, businessman, businesswoman

businessmen say **business people** or the **business community** if that is what you mean

Bussell, Darcey British ballet dancer

but, however often redundant, and increasingly wrongly used to connect two compatible statements; "in contrast, however, … " is tautologous

Butlins but **Pontin's**

butterflies lc, painted lady, red admiral, etc; but note **queen of Spain fritillary**

buyout but **buy-in**

byelection, bylaw, bypass, bystander

cabin attendant, flight attendant, cabin crew, cabin staff not air hostess, stewardess

cabinet, shadow cabinet

Cádiz

caesarean section

Caesars Palace no apostrophe

Cafcass Children and Family Court Advisory and Support Service

cafe no accent

Californian a person; the adjective is California, or Brian Wilson would have written about "Californian Girls"

Calor TM

Campari TM

Canary Wharf the whole development, not the main tower, which is No 1 Canada Square

cannabis people smoke cannabis rather than "experiment" with it, despite what politicians and young members of the royal family might claim

Canute (c994 1035) Danish king of England, Denmark and Norway who commanded the tide to turn back, so the legend says, to prove to his toadying courtiers that he was not all-powerful

canvas tent, painting
canvass solicit votes

capitals
Times have changed since the days of medieval manuscripts with elaborate hand-illuminated capital letters, or Victorian documents in which not just

proper names, but virtually all nouns were given initial caps (a Tradition valiantly maintained to this day by Estate Agents). A glance at the Guardian of, say, 1990, 1970 and 1950 would show greater use of capitals the further back you went. The tendency towards lower case, which in part reflects a less formal, less deferential society, has been accelerated by the explosion of the internet: some net companies, and many email users, have dispensed with capitals altogether.

Our style reflects these developments. We aim for coherence and consistency, but not at the expense of clarity. As with any aspect of style, it is impossible to be wholly consistent — there are almost always exceptions, so if you are unsure check for an individual entry in this guide. But here are the main principles:

jobs all lc, eg prime minister, US secretary of state, editor of the Guardian, readers' editor

titles differentiate between title and job description, eg the Archbishop of Canterbury, Rowan Williams, at first mention, thereafter Dr Williams or the archbishop; President Bush (but the US president, George Bush, and Mr Bush on subsequent mention); the Duke of Westminster (the duke at second mention); the Pope; the Queen

British government departments of state initial caps, eg Home Office, Foreign Office, Ministry of Defence (MoD on second mention). *See departments of state for a full list*

other countries lc, eg US state department, Russian foreign ministry

government agencies, commissions, public bodies, quangos, etc initial caps, eg Benefits Agency, Crown Prosecution Service, Customs and Excise, Equal Opportunities Commission, Heritage Lottery Fund, Parole Board

acts of parliament initial caps (but bills lc), eg Official Secrets Act, Criminal Justice Act 1992

parliamentary committees, reports and inquiries all lc, eg trade and industry select committee, Lawrence report, royal commission on electoral reform

artistic and cultural initial caps for names of institutions, etc, eg British Museum, Tate Modern, Royal Court, Leeds Castle, National Theatre, Blenheim Palace

churches, hospitals and schools cap up the proper or placename, lc the rest eg St Peter's church, Pembury, Great Ormond Street children's hospital, Ripon grammar school, Vernon county primary school

universities and colleges of further and higher education caps for institution, lc for departments, eg Sheffield University department of medieval and modern history, Oregon State University, Free University of Berlin, University of Queensland school of journalism, London College of Printing

geographical features, bridges lc, eg river Thames, the Wash, Sydney harbour, Golden Gate bridge, Monterey peninsula,

'I am a poet.
I distrust anything that starts with a capital letter'

Antjie Krog

Bondi beach, Solsbury hill (but Mount Everest)

words and phrases based on proper names that have lost connection with their origins (alsatian, cardigan, champagne, french windows, yorkshire pudding and numerous others) are usually lc; many are listed individually in this guide, as are the few exceptions (eg Long Island Iced tea)

cappuccino

car bomb

carcass plural **carcasses**

cards scratchcard, smartcard, swipecard, but credit card, debit card

careen to sway or keel over to one side; often confused with **career**, to rush along

career girl, career woman these labels are banned

carer an unpaid family member, partner or friend who helps a disabled or frail person with the activities of daily living; not someone who works in a caring job or profession. The term is important because carers are entitled to a range of benefits and services that depend on them recognising themselves as carers

Caribbean

carmaker

cashmere fabric

castoff one word (noun, adjective)
cast off two words (verb)

casual (workers) use freelance

Catalonia adjective **Catalan**

catchphrase

catch-22 lc unless specifically referring to Joseph Heller's novel Catch-22

cathedrals cap up, eg Canterbury Cathedral

Catholic church

caviar not caviare

CD, CDs, CD-rom

ceasefire

Ceausescu, Nicolae former president of Romania, deposed and executed in 1989

celibate, celibacy strictly refer to being unmarried (especially for religious reasons), but it is now acceptable to use them to mean abstaining from sexual intercourse

celsius scale of temperature invented by a man named Celsius; write with fahrenheit equivalent in brackets: 23C (73F), -3C (27F), etc (avoid "centigrade" because of its possible confusion with the 100th part of a grade). Each degree of increase in celsius is 1.8 in fahrenheit. *See numeracy*

Celtic not Glasgow Celtic

censor prevent publication
censure criticise severely

Center Parcs

centre on or in **revolve** around

century sixth century, 21st century, etc

CFC chlorofluorocarbon

chablis wines are lc, whether named after a place (as in this case) or a grape variety

chair acceptable in place of **chairman** or **chairwoman**, being nowadays widely used in the public sector and by organisations such as the Labour party and trade unions (though not the Conservative party, which had a "chairman" in kitten heels); if it seems inappropriate for a particular body, use a different construction ("the meeting was chaired by Alan" or "Georgina was in the chair")

champagne

chancellor of the duchy of Lancaster

chancellor of the exchequer

Channel 4, Channel Five but **Five** at second mention

Channel tunnel never Chunnel

chaos theory not a synonym for chaos. It describes the behaviour of dynamic systems that are sensitively dependent on their initial conditions. An example is the weather: under the "butterfly effect", the flap of a butterfly's wing in Brazil can in principle result in a tornado in Texas

chardonnay lc, like other wines, whether named after a grape (as in this case) or a region

chargé d'affaires

Charity Commission

chassis singular and plural

chateau, chateaux no accent

chatroom, chatshow

Chechnya inhabited by **Chechens**

checkout noun, adjective **check out** verb

cheese normally lc: **brie, camembert, cheddar, cheshire, double gloucester, lancashire, stilton**, etc, but uc for those still closely associated with a place, eg **Wensleydale**

cherubim plural of cherub

chicken tikka masala Britain's favourite dish

chief ("planning chiefs", etc): try to use proper job descriptions; officers or officials may be preferable

chief constable a job, not a title — John Smith, chief

constable of Greater Manchester; Mr Smith at second mention

chief secretary to the Treasury

chief whip

childcare, childminder

Chinese names
Mainland China: in two parts, eg Mao Zedong, Zhou Enlai, Jiang Zemin

Hong Kong, Taiwan: in two parts with hyphen, eg Tung Chee-hwa, Chiang Kai-shek (exception: when a building, park or the like is named after a person it becomes three parts, eg Chiang Kai Shek Cultural Centre); note also that Korean names are written the same way, eg Kim Il-sung

Singapore, Malaysia: in three parts, eg Lee Kuan Yew

For people with Chinese names elsewhere in the world, follow their preference — but make sure you know which is the surname

chock-a-block

Chomsky, Noam US linguist and political theorist

chords musical **cords** vocal

christened, christening use only when referring to a Christian

baptism: don't talk about a boat being christened or a football club christening a new stadium. *See Christian name*

Christian, Christianity but **unchristian**

Christian name use **first name** or **forename**

Christian Union an evangelical Christian organisation

Christie's

Christmas Day, Christmas Eve

chronic means lasting for a long time or constantly recurring, too often misused when acute (short but severe) is meant

Chumbawamba not Chumbawumba

church lc for the established church, eg "the church is no longer relevant today"; Catholic church, Anglican church, etc, but Church of England

cinemagoer

city in Britain a town that has been granted a charter by the crown; it usually has a cathedral **City** capped when used as shorthand for the City of London

civil servant, civil service

CJD Creutzfeldt-Jakob disease, not normally necessary to spell it out; it is acceptable to refer to variant CJD as the human form of BSE, but not as "the human form of mad cow disease"

classical music Mozart's 41st Symphony (or Symphony No 41) in C, K551; Rachmaninov's Piano Concerto No 2; Schubert's Sonata in A minor for Piano, D845

clearcut

cliches
Overused words and phrases to be avoided include: back burner, boost (massive or otherwise), bouquets and brickbats, but hey … , drop-dead gorgeous, insisted, luvvies, major, massive, political correctness, politically correct, PC, raft of measures, special, to die for, upsurge (surge will do); verbs overused in headlines include: bid, boost, fuel, hike, signal, target, set to.

A survey by the Plain English Campaign in 2004 found that the most irritating phrase in the language was "at the end of the day", followed by (in order of annoyance): at this moment in time, like (as in, like, this), with all due respect, to be perfectly honest with you, touch base, I hear what you're saying, going forward, absolutely, and blue sky thinking; other words and phrases that upset people included 24/7, ballpark figure, bottom line, diamond geezer, it's not rocket science, ongoing, prioritise, pushing the envelope, singing from the same hymn sheet, and thinking outside the box

cliffhanger

climbdown noun
climb down verb

cloud cuckoo land

coalfield, coalmine, coalminer

Coalite TM

coastguard

Coca-Cola, Coke TM

cockney

coconut

cold war

Coliseum London theatre
Colosseum Rome

collective nouns
Nouns such as committee, family, government, jury, take a singular verb or pronoun when thought of as a single unit, but a

plural verb or pronoun when thought of as a collection of individuals:

The committee gave its unanimous approval to the plans;

The committee enjoyed biscuits with their tea

The family can trace its history back to the middle ages;

The family were sitting down, scratching their heads

College of Arms

colleges take initial caps, eg Fire Service College; but not when college forms part of the name of a school, eg Bash Street sixth-form college, Eton college

Colombia South American country that we frequently misspell as "Columbia"

colon
Use like this: "to deliver the goods that have been invoiced in the preceding words" (Fowler).

This, from the paper, is a dreadful (but by no means isolated) example of the tendency to use a semicolon where only a colon will do: "Being a retired soap 'treasure' must be a bit like being in the army reserves; when a ratings war breaks out, it's time to dust off your uniform and wait by the phone"

colonel Colonel Napoleon Bogey, subsequently Col Bogey

Columbia as in District of Columbia (Washington DC) and Columbia University (New York)

Columbus Day October 12, marking the date Christopher Columbus landed in the West Indies in 1492; Columbus is also the state capital of Ohio

comedian male and female; do not use comedienne

'I am about to – or I am going to – die; either expression is used'

Last words of the 17th-century French Jesuit grammarian
Dominique Bouhours

commas
"The editor, Alan Rusbridger, is a man of great vision" — correct (commas) if there is only one

"The subeditor David Marsh is all style and no substance" — correct (no commas) if there are more than one

commented avoid, "she said" not "she commented"

Commons, House of Commons but the house, not the House

Commons committees lc, home affairs select committee, public accounts committee, etc

common sense noun **commonsense** adjective: "William Hague's 'commonsense revolution' showed little common sense"

Commonwealth, the

Commonwealth War Graves Commission

communique no accent

communism, communist lc, except in name of party: **Communist party**

company names
A tricky area, as so many companies these days have adopted unconventional typography and other devices that, in some cases, turn their names into logos. In general, we use the names that the companies use themselves: easyJet, eBay, ebookers, iSoft Group, Yahoo! are fine; but Adidas (not adidas), BhS (no italicised H), Toys Я Us (do not attempt to turn the R backwards). Many of these look odd, particularly when used as first word in a headline, although some are becoming more familiar with time

compare to/with
The former means liken to, the latter means make a comparison: so unless you are specifically likening someone or something to someone or something else, use compare with.

The lord chancellor compared himself to Cardinal Wolsey because he believed he was like Wolsey; I might compare him with Wolsey to assess their relative merits

compass points lc for regions: the north, the south of England, the south-west, north-east England; the same applies to geopolitical areas: the west, western Europe, the far east, south-east Asia, central America, etc; cap up, however, when part of the name of a county (West Sussex, East Riding of Yorkshire) or province (East Java, North Sulawesi, etc); note the following: East End, West End (London), Middle East, Latin America, North America, South America

Competition Commission

complement/compliment/ complimentary to complement is to make complete: the two strikers complemented each other; to compliment is to praise; a complimentary copy is free

complete or **finish** is better than finalise

comprise to consist of; "comprise of" is wrong

Concord town in Massachusetts **Concorde** plane

Congo acceptable on second mention for the Democratic Republic of the Congo (or DRC, formerly Zaire); we call its neighbour **Congo-Brazzaville**; never write "the Congo" unless referring to the river

Congregational uc when referring to the Congregational Union of England and Wales, formed in 1832, which joined the Presbyterian Church of England in 1972 to form the United Reformed Church

Congress (US)

conjoined twins not Siamese twins

connection not connexion

Conservative central office

Conservative party

consortium plural **consortiums**

constitution

Consuelo not Consuela; from a reader: "I really have had enough of show-off ignoramuses messing up my name. Consuelo is a Spanish abstract noun, masculine, invariable. Pilar and Mercedes are also Spanish female names derived, like Consuelo, from titles of the Virgin Mary"

consult not consult with

consumer price index (CPI) normally no need to spell it out

Consumers' Association

contemporary of the same period, though often wrongly used to mean modern; a performance of Shakespeare in contemporary dress would involve Elizabethan costume, not 21st-century clothes

continent, the mainland Europe

continual refers to things that happen repeatedly but not constantly
continuous indicates an unbroken sequence

contractions

Do not overuse contractions such as aren't, can't, couldn't, hasn't, don't, I'm, it's, there's and what's (even the horrific "there've" has appeared in the paper); while they might make a piece more colloquial or easier to read, they can be an irritant and a distraction, and make a serious article sound frivolous

convince/persuade having convinced someone of the facts, you might persuade them to do something

convener not convenor

conversions

We give metric measures and convert on first mention only to imperial in brackets (exceptions: miles and pints); if a rough figure is given in metric, do not convert it into an exact figure in imperial, and vice versa, eg if someone says the towns are about 50km apart, convert to 30 miles, not 31.07 miles; the same goes for rough amounts of currencies,

though don't round up £3.6bn to £4bn

cooperate, cooperation, cooperative no hyphen, but the store is the **Co-op**

coordinate

Le Corbusier (1887-1965) Swiss architect and city planner

cords vocal **chords** musical

Córdoba

cornish pasty

coronavirus

corporation of London

corps de ballet

cortege no accent

La Coruña

coruscating means sparkling, or emitting flashes of light; people seem to think, wrongly, that it means the same as excoriating, which means censuring severely eg "a coruscating attack on Blair's advisers"

councils lc apart from placename: Lancaster city council, London borough of Southwark, Kent county council

count 'em
Resist the temptation to use this
cliche, often seen in parenthesis
after a number is mentioned,
eg "the seminal Andrex puppy
advent calendar with 25 —
count 'em — puppy pictures"

counter-attack

coupe no accent

court martial
plural **courts martial**

court of St James's

courts all lc: court of appeal,
high court, supreme court,
magistrates court (no apostrophe),
European court of human rights,
international criminal court

couscous

crescendo a gradual increase
in loudness or intensity; musically
or figuratively, it is the build-up
to a climax, not the climax itself
(we frequently get this wrong)

cricket leg-side, leg-spinner,
off-spin, off-stump, silly mid-on,
mid-off, etc, all hyphenated

cripple, crippled offensive
and outdated; do not use

criterion plural **criteria**

Crombie TM

Crowley, Aleister dead
satanist

crown, the crown estate,
crown jewels

crucifixion, the

Crufts

cruise missile

Crusades, the

Cruz, Penélope

cubism, cubist

cumberland sausage

Cummings, EE US poet
(1894-1962) who, despite what
many people think, used capitals
in his signature

cunt *see swearwords*

Cup, FA after first mention it is
the Cup; but other cups are lc on
second mention

curb restrain **kerb** pavement

currencies
When the whole word is used it is
lc: euro, pound, sterling, dong, etc.
    Abbreviate dollars like this: $50
(US dollars); A$50 (Australian

dollars); HK$50 (Hong Kong dollars).

Convert all foreign amounts to sterling in brackets at first mention, but use common sense — there is no need to put £660,000 in brackets after the phrase "I feel like a million dollars"

currently "now" is usually preferable, if needed at all

cusp a place where two points meet (eg "on the cusp of Manchester and Salford"); sometimes misused to mean on the brink ("a girl on the cusp of womanhood")

custody since the 1989 Children Act the correct term for what used to be known as custody in cases involving care of children is **residence**

Customs, Customs and Excise, HM Customs (all singular) but **customs officers**

cutbacks avoid; **cuts** will suffice

cyberspace

Czech Republic

dadaism, dadaist

Dalí, Salvador (1904-89)
Spanish surrealist

dancefloor

dangling participles
Avoid constructions such as
"having died, they buried him";
the pitfalls are nicely highlighted
in Mark Lawson's novel Going
Out Live, in which a TV critic
writes: "Dreary, repetitive and
well past the sell-by date, I
switched off the new series of
Fleming Faces"

dark ages

dashes
Beware sentences — such as
this one — that dash about all
over the place — commas (or
even, very occasionally, brackets)
are often better; semicolons also
have their uses

data takes a singular verb (like

agenda); though strictly a plural,
no one ever uses "agendum" or
"datum"

dates
January 1 2000 (no commas);
it is occasionally alleged that
putting month before date in
this way is an "Americanisation"
— in which case it should be
pointed out that this has been
our style since the first issue of
the Manchester Guardian on
May 5 1821.
    21st century; fourth century
BC; AD2006 but 1000BC; for
decades use figures: the
swinging 60s or 1960s

daughter of, son of
Think twice before using these
terms: often only the person's
father is described and such
descriptions can smack of
snobbery as well as sexism.
Simplistic labels may also be
misleading: we published a
clarification after calling Captain
James Cook the son of a

Scottish farm labourer. True
enough, but Cook's mother was
a Yorkshire woman and he is a
famous son of Yorkshire

Davison, Emily suffragette
who died after falling under
George V's horse at the 1913
Derby

Day-Glo TM

daylong but **month-long,
year-long**

D-day

D notices issued by the
defence, press and broadcasting
advisory committee "suggesting"
that the media do not publish
sensitive information

death row

debacle no accents

debatable

decades use figures if you
abbreviate: roaring 20s, swinging
60s, etc

defensible

deforestation

defuse render harmless
diffuse spread about

deja vu no accents

delphic

delusion/illusion "That the
sun moves round the Earth was
once a delusion, and is still an
illusion" (Fowler)

DeMille, Cecil B (1881-1959)
Hollywood producer and director

Democratic party (US), not
"Democrat party"

Dench, Dame Judi not Judy

De Niro, Robert

denouement no accent

departments of state
British government ministries
(but not ministers) take initial
caps as follows:
Cabinet Office (but the cabinet)
Department for
  Constitutional Affairs
Department for Culture,
  Media and Sport
Department for Education
  and Skills
Department for Environment,
  Food and Rural Affairs
  (Defra on second mention)
Department of Health
Department for International
  Development
Department of Trade and
  Industry (DTI on second
  mention)

Department for Transport
Department for Work and
  Pensions
Foreign Office
Home Office
Ministry of Defence (MoD on
  second mention)
Northern Ireland Office
Office of the Deputy Prime
  Minister
Scotland Office (not Scottish
  Office)
Treasury
Wales Office (not Welsh Office)
  lc when departments are
abbreviated, eg **environment
department, transport
department**
  lc for departments and
ministries of other countries, eg
**US state department, Iraqi
foreign ministry**

dependant noun
dependent adjective

dependence

depositary person
depository place

de rigueur the two Us are
de rigueur

Derry, Co Derry not
Londonderry

descendants come after
ancestors; you wouldn't think the
Guardian would get this simple
thing wrong as often as we do

deselect

desiccate

despoil, despoliation

dessert pudding, but **just
deserts**

detente no accent

Dettol TM

developing countries use
this term in preference to "third
world"

devil, the

DeVito, Danny

Diabetes UK formerly known
as the British Diabetic
Association

dialects cockney, estuary
English, geordie, scouse

DiCaprio, Leonardo

Dictaphone TM

diehard

dietician

different from or **to**, not
different than

dignitary, dignitaries

dilapidated not delapidated

dilettante

dim sum

Dinky Toys TM

diphtheria

diplomatic service

direct speech
People we write about are
allowed to speak in their own,
not necessarily the Guardian's,
style, but be sensitive: do not,
for example, expose someone
to ridicule for dialect or
grammatical errors. Do not
attempt facetious phonetic
renditions such as "oop north",
"fooking" and "booger" when
interviewing someone from the
north, or "dahn sarf" when
writing about south London

director general

disabled people not "the
disabled".
  Use positive language about
disability, avoiding outdated
terms that stereotype or
stigmatise. Terms to avoid,
with acceptable alternatives
in brackets, include victim of,
crippled by, suffering from,
afflicted by (prefer person who
has, person with); wheelchair-
bound, in a wheelchair (uses
a wheelchair); invalid (disabled
person); mentally handicapped,
backward, retarded, slow
(person with learning difficulties);
the disabled, the handicapped,
the blind, the deaf (disabled
people, blind people, deaf
people); deaf and dumb (deaf
and speech-impaired, hearing
and speech-impaired)

discernible not discernable

discolour but **discoloration**

discomfit thwart; do not
confuse with **discomfort**, make
uncomfortable

discreet circumspect
discrete separate

disfranchise not
disenfranchise

disinterested free from bias, objective (the negative form of interested as in "interested party"); **uninterested** not taking an interest (the negative form of interested as in "interested in football")

dispatch, dispatch box (Commons), not despatch

Disprin TM, use aspirin

disk (computers), not disc

Disneyland Paris formerly Euro Disney

dissociate, dissociation not disassociate, disassociation

divorcee a divorced person, male or female

Doctor Who the title of the series; the character's name is **the Doctor**, and it should never be abbreviated to Dr Who

dogs lc, alsatian, doberman, labrador, rottweiler, yorkshire terrier; but Irish setter, old English sheepdog

D'oh! as Homer Simpson would say, note the apostrophe

Dolby TM

dome, the Millennium Dome at first mention, thereafter the dome

Dominica lies in the Windward Islands, south-west of the Dominican Republic

Dominican Republic shares an island with Haiti

Donahue, Phil

dos and don'ts

Dostoevsky, Fyodor Mikhailovich (1821-81) Russian novelist

dotcom

double, the as in Sheffield United may win the double (FA Cup and Premiership)

dover sole

downmarket

Down's syndrome

dozen precisely, not approximately, 12

Dr use at second mention for academic, medical and scientific doctors and doctors of divinity, not, for example, a politician who happens to have a PhD in history

draconian

draftsman of document
draughtsman of drawing

dreamed not dreamt

dressing room two words

driving licence not driver's licence

drug companies, drug dealer, drug raid, drug squad, drug tsar not drugs raid, etc

drug enforcement administration (US, not agency), DEA at second mention

drum'n'bass

drunkenness

dub avoid tabloidese such as "they have been dubbed the nation's leading experts on style" (even if true)

due to/owing to
Many people ignore this distinction, but it can be valuable. For example, compare "It was difficult to assess the changes due to outside factors" with "It was difficult to assess the changes owing to outside factors". The first says the changes that were a result of outside factors were difficult to assess, the second says outside factors made the changes difficult to assess (if in doubt, **because of** can be substituted for owing to, but not due to)

'The most valuable of all talents is that of never using two words when one will do'

Thomas Jefferson

dugout

Duke of Westminster or wherever, first mention; thereafter the duke

Duke of York first mention; thereafter Prince Andrew or the prince

dumb do not use; say speech-impaired

du Pré, Jacqueline (1945-87) English cellist, Du Pré at second mention

Dupré, Marcel (1886-1971) French organist and composer

dyke not dike

dynamo plural **dynamos**

Dynamo football teams from the former Soviet Union are Dynamo; teams from Romania are **Dinamo**

dyslexia write "Paul has dyslexia" rather than labelling him "a dyslexic" or saying he "suffers from" dyslexia

earlier often redundant as context will inform the reader: "They met this month" is preferable to "They met earlier this month" and will save space

Earls Court no apostrophe

earring

earshot

Earth in an astronomical context; but moon, sun

East Anglia

east coast mainline

East End inner east London north of the river (the equivalent district south of the Thames is south-east London)

EastEnders TV soap

Easter Day not Easter Sunday

eastern Europe, western Europe

East Jerusalem

East Riding of Yorkshire council

easyJet

eBay

ebook

eccles cake

E coli

e-commerce

ecstasy (drug), lc

ecu European currency unit, superseded by the euro

Edinburgh festival, Edinburgh Fringe festival

educationist not educationalist

eerie weird; **Erie** North American lake; **eyrie** of eagles

effect/affect *see affect*

effectively not a synonym for in effect: "the Blair campaign was launched effectively in 1992" means the intended effect was achieved; "the Blair campaign was in effect launched in 1992" means this was not the official launch, but the event described did have the effect of launching it, whether intended or not. The word effectively is overused as well as misused, and can often be omitted

effete does not mean effeminate or foppish, but "weak, ineffectual or decadent as a result of over-refinement … exhausted, worn out, spent" (Collins)

efit (electronic facial identification technique) program used to create police drawings

eg no full point

Eid al-Adha (Festival of Sacrifice) Muslim festival laid down in Islamic law, celebrates the end of the hajj. Note that eid means festival, so it is tautologous to describe it as the "Eid festival"

Eid al-Fitr Muslim festival of thanksgiving laid down in Islamic law, celebrates the end of Ramadan (al-fitr means "the breaking of the fast")

eid mubarak not a festival but a greeting (mubarak means "may it be blessed")

Eire do not use; say Republic of Ireland or Irish Republic

elan no accent

ElBaradei, Mohamed director general of the International Atomic Energy Agency, Dr ElBaradei after first mention

elderly do not use to describe anyone under 70

El Dorado fabled city of gold
Eldorado fabled flop of a soap

electrocution death by electric shock, so don't say survivors of torture were "electrocuted" during their ordeal — rather that they were given electric shocks

elegiac

elite

ellipsis use spaces before and after ellipses, eg "She didn't want to go there … "; there is no need for a full point

email

emanate is intransitive; use

exude if you need a transitive verb

Embankment, the London

embargo plural **embargos**

embarrass, embarrassment

embassy lc, eg British embassy

emigrate leave a country **immigrate** arrive in one

emir not amir

employment tribunal not industrial tribunal

EMS European monetary system

Emu economic and monetary union

enamoured of not by or with

enclose not inclose

enervate to deprive of strength or vitality

enforce, enforceable

England, English take care not to offend by saying England or English when you mean Britain or British. *See Scotland*

English Heritage, English Nature, English Partnerships

en masse

enormity something monstrous or wicked; not synonymous with large

enrol, enrolling, enrolment

en route not on route

ensure make certain; **insure** against risk; **assure** life

enthral, enthralling

entr'acte

epicentre the point on the earth's surface directly above the focus of an earthquake or underground explosion; frequently misused to mean the centre or focus itself

epilepsy we do not define people by their medical condition: seizures are epileptic, people are not; so say (if relevant) "Mr Smith, who has epilepsy …" not "Mr Smith, an epileptic …"

EPO erythropoietin, a performance-enhancing drug

equator, the

ere long not e'er long

ERM exchange rate mechanism

Ernie electronic random number indicator equipment: the machine that picks winning premium bond numbers

Eskimo is a language spoken in Greenland, Canada, Alaska and Siberia. Please note that it has no more words for snow than does English. The people are **Inuit** (singular **Inuk**), not "Eskimos"

espresso not expresso

establishment, the

estuary English

Eta not ETA

ethnic never say ethnic when you mean ethnic minority, which leads to such nonsense as "the constituency has a small ethnic population"

ethnic cleansing do not use as a euphemism for genocide unless in quote marks

EU European Union (no need to spell out at first mention); formerly EC (European Community); before that EEC (European Economic Community)

Euan, Ewan or Ewen?
Euan Blair
Ewan McGregor
Ewen Bremner, Ewen MacAskill

euro currency; plural **euros** and **cents**

Euro do not use as a prefix to everything European, but Euro-MP is an acceptable alternative to MEP

Euro Disney now called **Disneyland Paris**

Europe includes Britain, so don't say, for example, something is common "in Europe" unless it is common in Britain as well; to distinguish between Britain and the rest of Europe the phrase "continental Europe" may be useful; **eastern Europe, central Europe, western Europe**

euroland, eurozone

European commission the commission after first mention

European convention on human rights

European court of human rights nothing to do with the EU; it is a Council of Europe body

Eurosceptic one word, capped: they are sceptics about the EU, not just the euro

Eurovision song contest

evangelical fundamentalist wing of Christianity; **evangelist** someone who spreads the gospel

every day noun and adverb: it happens every day; **everyday** adjective: an everyday mistake

every parent's nightmare cliche; from a reader: "This seems to crop up for anything to do with children, from abduction, to death, to today's piece on musical taste. As a parent I can't cope with that many nightmares"

exchequer, the

exclusive term used by tabloid newspapers to denote a story that is in all of them

execution the carrying out of a death sentence by lawful authority, so a terrorist, for example, does not "execute" someone

ex officio by right of position or office

ex parte on behalf of one party only

expat, expatriate not ex-pat or expatriot; this is "ex" meaning "out of" (as in export, extract), not "ex-" meaning "former" (as in ex-husband)

explained avoid; write "he said" not "he explained"

Export Credits Guarantee Department ECGD at second mention

extraterrestrial, extraterritorial

extrovert not extravert

eye level no hyphen

eyewitness one word, but **witness** is preferable

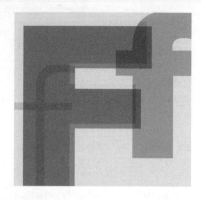

facade no cedilla

factoid not a trivial fact, but a mistaken assumption repeated so often that it is believed to be true (a word coined by Norman Mailer)

FA Cup the Cup (the cap C is hallowed by convention); all other cups lc at second mention

fahrenheit 68F etc, use in brackets after celsius figure

Fáilte Ireland Ireland's tourism authority

fairytale

falafel

fallout

far, farther, farthest of distances, otherwise **further, furthest**

far east but **Middle East**

farrago a hotchpotch or jumbled mixture, not synonymous with **fiasco** (a humiliating failure)

Farsi language spoken by the majority of Iranians (not Persian)

fascism, fascist

fashion weeks lc, eg London fashion week

fatality use death

father of two, etc, not father-of-two

fatwa an edict, not necessarily a death sentence

Al Fayed, Mohamed owner of Harrods (Mr Fayed after first mention); the son who died in Paris in 1997 was Dodi Fayed

faze disconcert **phase** a stage

FBI Federal Bureau of Investigation, no need to spell out

fedayeen Arab fighters (the word means those who risk their lives for a cause); can be capped up when referring to a specific force, eg the Saddam Fedayeen militia that fought coalition forces in the 2003 Iraq war

Federal Reserve Board first reference, **the Fed** thereafter

fed up with not fed up of

feelgood factor

fellow lc, eg a fellow of All Souls, fellow artist, fellow members, etc (and do not hyphenate)

ferris wheel

festivals lc, eg Cannes film festival, Edinburgh Fringe festival

fete no accent

fewer/less fewer means smaller in number, eg fewer coins; less means smaller in quantity, eg less money

Ffestiniog

fiance male **fiancee** female; but note **divorcee** is both male and female

Fianna Fáil Irish political party

field marshal

'There's nothing to it, really ... it's just a matter of checking the facts and the spelling, crossing out the first sentence, and removing any attempts at jokes'

Michael Frayn
Towards the End of the Morning

figures spell out from one to nine; integers from 10 to 999,999; thereafter 1m, 3.2bn (except for people and animals, eg 2 million viewers, 8 billion cattle)

film-maker

Filofax TM; use **personal organiser** unless you are sure

finalise, finalised avoid, use **complete, completed** or **finish, finished**

Financial Services Authority
FSA on second mention

financial years 2004-05, etc

Fine Gael Irish political party

fine-tooth comb

Finnegans Wake

firebomb

firefighter not fireman

firing line the people who do the firing; if they are aiming at you, you are in the line of fire not "in the firing line"

firm strictly a partnership without limited liability, such as solicitors or accountants, but may be used in place of "company" in headlines

first, second, third spell out up to ninth, then 10th, 21st, millionth

firstly, secondly prefer first, second, etc

first aid

first-hand

first minister (Scottish parliament, Welsh assembly, Northern Ireland assembly)

first name, forename not Christian name

first world war

flak not flack

flammable means the same as **inflammable**; the negative is **non-flammable**

flaunt/flout to flaunt is to make a display of something, as in flaunting wealth; to flout is to show disregard for something, as in flouting the seatbelt law

fledgling not fledgeling

flounder/founder to flounder is to perform a task badly, like someone stuck in mud; founder means fail: a business might be foundering because its bosses are floundering

flu

fluky not flukey

flyer not flier

fo'c'sle abbreviation of forecastle

focus, focused, focusing

foetid not fetid

foetus not fetus

fogey not fogy

following prefer after, eg Mansfield Town went to pieces after their Cup exit

foot and mouth disease

forbear abstain
forebear ancestor

foreign names
The French (or French origin) le or de, the Italian di and the Dutch van are all lc when the name is full out: eg Graeme le Saux, Roberto di Matteo, Pierre van Hooijdonk; but Le Saux, Di Matteo, Van Hooijdonk when written without forenames

foreign placenames
Style for foreign placenames evolves with common usage. Leghorn has become Livorno, and maybe one day München will supplant Munich, but not yet. Remember that many names have become part of the English language: Geneva is the English name for the city Switzerland's French speakers refer to as Genève and its German speakers call Genf.

Accordingly we opt for locally used names, with these main exceptions (the list is not exhaustive, apply common sense): Archangel, Basle, Berne, Brittany, Cologne, Dunkirk, Florence, Fribourg, Genoa, Gothenburg, Hanover, Kiev, Lombardy, Milan, Munich, Naples, Normandy, Nuremberg, Padua, Piedmont, Rome, Sardinia, Seville, Sicily, Syracuse, Turin, Tuscany, Venice, Zurich

And next time someone says we should call Burma "Myanmar" because that's what it calls itself, point out that Colonel Gadafy renamed Libya "The Great Socialist People's Libyan Arab Jamahiriyya"

foreign words and phrases
Italicise, with roman translation in brackets, if it really is a foreign word or phrase and not an anglicised one, in which case it is roman with no accents (exceptions: exposé, resumé).

Use accents on French, German, Spanish, and Irish Gaelic words.

But remember Orwell: do not use a foreign word where a suitable English equivalent exists

forensic belonging to the courts; does not mean scientific

forego go before
forgo go without

forever continually: he is forever changing his mind; **for ever** for always: I will love you for ever

former Soviet republics
These are:
  Armenia adjective **Armenian**
  Azerbaijan adjective
    Azerbaijani (though there are ethnic Azeris in, eg, Armenia)
  Belarus adjective **Belarussian**
  Estonia adjective **Estonian** (Estonia did not join the Commonwealth of Independent States)
  Georgia adjective **Georgian**
  Kazakhstan adjective **Kazakh**
  Kyrgyzstan adjective **Kyrgyz**
  Latvia adjective **Latvian** (not in the commonwealth)
  Lithuania adjective
    Lithuanian (not in the commonwealth)
  Moldova adjective **Moldovan**
  Russia adjective **Russian**
  Tajikistan adjective **Tajik**
  Turkmenistan adjective
    Turkmen (its citizens are Turkmen, singular Turkman)
  Ukraine adjective **Ukrainian** (not "the Ukraine")
  Uzbekistan adjective **Uzbek**

Formica TM

formula plural **formulas**, but **formulae** in scientific context

formula one motor racing

fortuitous by chance, accidental; not by good fortune, lucky

fosbury flop

Fourth of July

foxhunting

FRA fellow of the Royal Academy; **FRS** fellow of the Royal Society

fractions two-thirds, three-quarters, etc, but two and a half

Frankenstein the monster's creator, not the monster

Frankenstein food has already become a cliche to describe GM food: do not use

french fries, french kiss, french letter, french polish, french window

fresco plural **frescoes**

Freud, Lucian British artist, not Lucien

freudian slip

frontbench, frontline, frontrunner

FTSE 100

fuck do not describe this as "a good, honest old-fashioned Anglo-Saxon word" because, first, there is no such thing as an Anglo-Saxon word (they spoke Old English) and, more important, its first recorded use dates from 1278.
See swearwords

fuel overused as a verb

fulfil, fulfilling, fulfilment

fulsome means "cloying, excessive, disgusting by excess" (and is not, as some appear to believe, a clever word for full); so "fulsome praise" should not be used in a complimentary sense

fundraiser, fundraising

fungus plural **fungi**

Gadafy, Muammar Libyan president, Col Gadafy on second mention

gaff hook or spar, also slang for house; **blow the gaff** give away a secret; **gaffe** blunder

Gambia, the not Gambia

gambit an opening strategy that involves some sacrifice or concession; so to talk of an opening gambit is tautologous — an opening ploy might be better

gameplan, gameshow

Gandhi not Ghandi

García Lorca, Federico (1898-1936) Spanish writer

García Márquez, Gabriel Colombian novelist

Garda Irish police force; **garda** (plural **gardaí**) Irish police officer

garotte not garrotte or garrote

garryowen up-and-under (rugby union)
Garryowen Irish rugby club

gases plural of gas, not gasses

Gatt general agreement on tariffs and trade

gay use as an adjective, eg "gay bishops", "gay people", rather than a noun ("gays") where possible, though "gays and lesbians" is OK

Gaudí, Antoni (1852-1926) Catalan architect

Gauguin, Paul (1848-1903) French painter, often misspelt as Gaugin

Gaza Strip

Gb gigabits **GB** gigabytes

gender

Our use of language should reflect not only changes in society but the newspaper's values. Phrases such as career girl or career woman, for example, are outdated (more women have careers than men) and patronising (there is no male equivalent): never use them. Businessmen, housewives, male nurse, woman pilot, woman (or lady!) doctor similarly reinforce outdated stereotypes.

Actor and comedian cover men and women; not actress, comedienne (but waiter and waitress are acceptable — at least for the moment). Firefighter, not fireman; PC, not WPC (most police forces have abandoned the distinction).

Use humankind or humanity rather than mankind, a word that, as one of our readers points out, "alienates half the population from their own history".

Never say "his" to cover men and women: use his or her, or a different construction; in sentences such as "a teacher who beats his/her pupils is not fit to do the job", there is usually a way round the problem — in this case, "teachers who beat their pupils ..."

general General Tommy Franks at first mention, then Gen Franks

general election

General Medical Council
(GMC), doctors' disciplinary body

Geneva convention

geography distinct areas are capped up: Black Country, East Anglia, Lake District, Midlands, Peak District, West Country; but areas defined by compass points are lc: the north, the south-east, the south-west, etc

german measles but **rubella** is preferable

ghetto plural **ghettoes**

ghoti George Bernard Shaw's proposed spelling of the word "fish" (gh as in trough, o as in women, ti as in nation)

Gibraltar overseas territory or dependency, not a British colony

gift not a verb (unless, perhaps, directly quoting a football manager or player: "We gifted Spurs their second goal")

girl female under 18

girlie noun (only when quoting someone); **girly** adjective (eg girly clothes); **girlish** behaviour

girlfriend

Giscard d'Estaing, Valéry former French president, Mr Giscard on second mention

Giuliani, Rudolph or Rudy former New York mayor (not "Rudi")

Giuseppe regularly misspelt as Guiseppe

GLA A mistake repeated ad nauseam is the assumption that GLA stands for "Greater London assembly". There is no such thing. The **Greater London authority** constitutes the mayor, who runs it, and the **London assembly**, which holds the mayor to account

glamorous not glamourous

Glasgow kiss

glasnost

GM crops, GM food no need to write genetically modified in full at first mention

GMT Greenwich mean time: the ship ran aground at 8am local time (0700 GMT)

goalline, goalpost

gobsmacked use only when directly quoting someone

God

godchild, goddaughter, godfather, godmother, godson

Goldsmiths College no apostrophe

golf for holes, use numbers: 1st, 2nd, 18th, etc; matchplay: one word, except World Match Play Championship; the Open not the British Open

Good Friday agreement

goodness, for goodness sake

goodnight

go-slow noun **go slow** verb

government lc in all contexts and all countries; resist the awful trend to say, for eg, "Lord Browne fended off accusations of

being too close to government"
— it is **the government**

government departments
see departments of state

graffiti is plural, **graffito** is the
singular

grammar the set of rules
followed by speakers of a
language, rather than a list of
arbitrary dos and don'ts, or
as Ambrose Bierce put it:
"a system of pitfalls thoughtfully
prepared for the feet of the
self-made man"

grandad but **granddaughter**

grandparents mention this
status only when relevant, leave
"battling grannies" and similar
examples of ageism and sexism
to the tabloids, in particular we
should avoid such patronising
drivel as "How this 55-year-old
granny came to earn $25m a
year" (in a page 1 blurb) — just
in case anyone still didn't get the
message the front of G2 said:
"She's five foot two, she's a
grandmother and she earns
$25m a year"

grand prix lc, the British grand
prix **grands prix** plural

grassroots one word

'A preschooler's
tacit knowledge
of **grammar**
is more
sophisticated
than the thickest
style manual'

Steven Pinker
The Language Instinct

Great Britain England, Wales
and Scotland; if you want to
include Northern Ireland, use
Britain or the UK

**great-grandfather,
great-great-grandmother**

green a green activist, the
green movement, but uc when
referring to so-named political
parties, eg the German Greens

green belt designated areas
around cities subject to strict
planning controls, not open
countryside in general

greenfield site one that has not been built on before; one that has been built on before is a **brownfield site**

greenhouse effect energy from the Earth's surface is trapped in the lower atmosphere by gases that prevent it leaking into space, a natural phenomenon that makes life possible, whose enhancement by natural or manmade means may make life impossible. Not the result of the hole in the ozone layer, whose thinning in the upper atmosphere is due to CFCs; the connection is that CFCs are also greenhouse gases

green paper

grisly gruesome **grizzly** bear

G7 Group of Seven leading industrial countries (Britain, Canada, France, Germany, Italy, Japan and the US), but no need to spell out

G8 the G7 plus Russia

Guantánamo Bay

guerrilla

Guevara, Che (1928-67) Argentinian-born revolutionary

Guildhall (City of London), not "the Guildhall"

Gulf, the not the Persian or Arabian Gulf

Gulf war of 1991

guinea pig

gun battle not gunbattle

guttural not gutteral

Gypsies uc, recognised as an ethnic group under the Race Relations Act, as are Irish Travellers

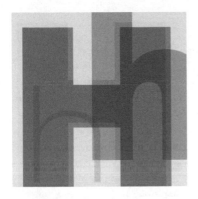

Ha'aretz Israeli newspaper

habeas corpus

Hair, Darrell Australian cricket umpire

Hague, The cap up; not "the Hague"

hajj

half normally no hyphen: half asleep, half dead, half past, half price; but hyphenate adjectival phrases such as a half-eaten sandwich

half a dozen

halfway, halfwit

Halloween

halo plural **haloes**

Hambros Bank

Hamed, Prince Naseem boxer, Hamed at second mention

Hamilton Academical not Academicals, nickname the Accies

handbill, handbook, handout

handicapped do not use to refer to people with disabilities or learning difficulties

hanging participles *see dangling participles*

Hanukah

happy-clappy derogatory term describing evangelical Christians, do not use

hara-kiri known less vulgarly in Japan as **seppuku**

harass, harassment

hardline adjective, **hardliner** noun, take a hard line

harebrained not hairbrained

hare lip never use, say **cleft lip** or **cleft palate**

Haringey north London borough, one ward of which is **Harringay**

Harrods

hat-trick

hazard/risk scientists use hazard to mean a potential for harm and risk to mean the actual probability of harm occurring; though headline writers may feel more at home with risk than hazard, the distinction is worth bearing in mind

headdress

headlines
Use active verbs where possible, particularly in news headlines: "Editors publish new style guidelines" is much better than "New style guidelines published". Avoid tabloidese such as bid, brand, dub, and slam, and broadsheet cliches such as insist, signal, and target.

Take care over ambuiguity: "Landmine claims dog UK arms firm", which appeared in the paper, contains so many ambiguous words that you have to read it several times to work out what it means.

Also to be avoided are quotation marks, unless essential to signify a quote or for legal reasons. And resist the temptation to replace "and" with a comma: "Blair and Brown agree euro deal" not "Blair, Brown agree euro deal".

Be careful when making references to popular culture: "Mrs Culpepper's lonely hearts club banned" works, because most people are familiar with Sgt Pepper's, but allusions to your favourite obscure 70s prog-rock album are likely to pass over most readers' heads. Long after everyone had forgotten the 60s movie Charlie Bubbles, tabloid sports subeditors continued to mystify readers by using the headline "Charlie bubbles" whenever Charlie Nicholas (or any other Charlie) scored a goal.

Puns are fine — "Where there's muck there's bras", about a farmer's wife who started a lingerie business, was voted 2003 headline of the year by our staff — but do not overuse, or resort to tired puns such as "flushed with success" (this story has got a plumber in it!). In the 70s the Guardian suffered from a reputation for excruciating puns; today, we want to be known for clever, original and witty headlines

headquarters can be used as a singular ("a large headquarters") or plural ("our headquarters are in London"); HQ, however, takes the singular

headteacher one word, not headmaster, headmistress; but **Association of Head Teachers**

Health and Safety Executive HSE on second mention

healthcare

Heathrow airport or simply Heathrow; not "London's Heathrow"

heaven

hectares not abbreviated, convert to acres in brackets at first mention

height in metres with imperial conversion, eg 1.68 metres (5ft 7in)

heir apparent someone certain to inherit from a deceased unless he or she dies first or is taken out of the will; don't use to mean "likely successor"

hell, hades

hello not hallo (and certainly not "hullo", unless quoting the Rev ARP Blair)

help help to decide or help decide; not "help and decide"

herculean

here generally avoid if what you mean is "in Britain"

Heritage Lottery Fund

Her Majesty the Queen is HM, never HRH

hiccup not hiccough

highfalutin

high flyer

highland fling

Highlands, the (Scottish)

high street lc in retail spending stories: "the recession is making an impact in the high street"; capped only in proper name: "I went shopping in Walthamstow High Street"

Highways Agency

hijab covering for the head and face worn by some Muslim women

hijack of movable objects only, not of schools, embassies, etc

hike a walk, not a rise in interest rates

hip-hop

hippopotamus plural
hippopotamuses

hippy plural **hippies**

His Master's Voice TM
(picture of Nipper the dog with
phonograph)

historian, historic use "a" not
"an", unless in a direct quote

hi-tech

HIV positive no hyphen

Hizbullah not Hezbollah

hoard/horde a hoard of
treasure; a horde (or hordes) of
tourists

Ho Chi Minh City formerly
Saigon

hoi polloi common people,
the masses; "the hoi polloi" is
acceptable

Holland do not use when you
mean the Netherlands, with the
exception of the Dutch football
team, who are conventionally
known as Holland

Holocaust

holy grail

Holy Land

homebuyer, homeowner
one word

home counties

homeopathy

homeland but **home town**

homepage

homogeneous uniform, of the
same kind; **homogenous**
(biology) having a common
descent; the latter is often
misused for the former

homosexual rape do not use;
say rape (or male rape if
necessary)

honeybee

Hong Kong names like
Taiwanese and Korean names,
Hong Kong names are written in
two parts with a hyphen, eg
Tung Chee-hwa

hon members of parliament

honorarium
plural **honorariums**

honorifics
On news and comment pages:
Tony Blair or Sir Bobby Charlton
at first mention, thereafter Mr

Blair, Sir Bobby, etc; in a big feature or news focus piece on a news page it may be appropriate to drop honorifics.

Use surnames only after first mention for sportsmen and sportswomen; for actors, authors, artists, musicians, etc; for journalists (but not for editors and television and radio executives); for those convicted of criminal offences; and for the dead (though use sensitivity: they are not stripped of their honorifics immediately — we would usually use them until after the funeral).

If people not normally given honorifics (eg footballers) are charged with criminal offences, they are given back their titles for the duration of the case. Similarly in court stories it sounds heartless and crude to write "Mr Radcliffe is charged with raping and murdering Jones, an 86 year old who lived alone in her flat in Kensal Rise".Restore the deceased's honorific in such reports.

Use Dr at second mention for academic, medical and scientific doctors and doctors of divinity.

In other sections: surnames are acceptable after first mention, but again use your judgment: for parents of a child who has drowned, say, surnames only may be inappropriate

Hoover TM; say **vacuum cleaner**

hopefully like many other adverbs, such as frankly, happily, honestly and sadly, hopefully can be used as a "sentence adverb" indicating the writer's view of events — "hopefully, we will reach the summit" — or as a "manner adverb" modifying a verb — "we set off hopefully for the summit". Why some people are upset by "hopefully we will win" and not "sadly we lost" is a mystery

horrendous sounds like a rather ugly combination of horrific and tremendous, but is in fact from the Latin for fearful; **horrific** is generally preferable

hospital use a not an

hospitalised avoid; use taken (never "rushed") to hospital

'An average English word is four letters and a half.

By hard, honest labour I've dug all the large words out of my vocabulary and shaved them down till the average is three and a half letters… I never write metropolis for seven cents because I can get the same money for city'

Mark Twain

hospitals cap the placename, eg Derby district general hospital, Great Ormond Street children's hospital, Royal London hospital; but London Clinic

hotdog

hotel use a not an

hotspot

houseboat, housebreaker, housebuyer, householder, housekeeper

Housing Corporation

housewife avoid

hovercraft

Hudson Bay but **Hudson's Bay Company**

humanity, humankind use instead of mankind. *See gender*

hummus you eat it
humus you put it on the garden

humour, humorist, humorous

hunky dory

hyperbole don't overegg stories: strive instead for straight and accurate reporting; Guardian readers prefer the unvarnished truth. *See sexing up*

hyphens

Our style is to use one word wherever possible, including some instances where a word might be hyphenated by other publications. Hyphens tend to clutter up text (particularly when the computer breaks already hyphenated words at the end of lines).

Inventions, ideas and new concepts often begin life as two words, then become hyphenated, before finally becoming accepted as one word. Why wait? "Wire-less" and "down-stairs" were once hyphenated. In pursuit of this it is preferable to go further than Collins does in many cases: eg trenchcoat is two words in Collins but one under our style; words such as handspring, madhouse and talkshow should all be one word, not two words, and not hyphenated.

Do use hyphens where not using one would be ambiguous, eg to distinguish "black-cab drivers come under attack" from "black cab-drivers come under attack".

Do not use after adverbs ending in -ly, eg politically naive, wholly owned, but hyphens are needed with short and common adverbs, eg ill-prepared report, hard-bitten hack, much-needed grammar lesson, well-established principle of style (note though that in the construction "the principle of style is well established" there is no need to hyphenate).

Finally, do use hyphens to form compound adjectives, eg two-tonne vessel, three-year deal, 19th-century artist

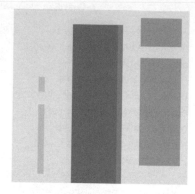

icon, iconic words in danger of losing all meaning after more than 1,000 appearances in the Guardian during 2003, lazily employed to describe anything vaguely memorable or well-known — from Weetabix, Dr Martens boots and the Ferrero Rocher TV ads to Jimi Hendrix's final gigs and the vacant fourth plinth in Trafalgar Square

ie no full points

IJ if a Dutch word starts with IJ then both letters are always capped (there is a waterway called the IJ so a lot of places have IJ in their name, eg IJsselmeer, IJmuiden, etc)

illegitimate do not use to refer to children born outside marriage (unless in a historical context, eg "the illegitimate son of Charles the Good")

iMac, iPod

immigrate to arrive in a country **emigrate** to leave one

immune to not immune from

Imperial College London no commas

impinge, impinging

impostor not imposter

impracticable impossible, it cannot be done **impractical** possible in theory but not workable at the moment

inchoate just beginning or undeveloped, not chaotic or disorderly

incident be wary of this word, another — "attack" or "clash", for example — will often stand better in its place; within a couple of years of the massacre in Tiananmen Square the Chinese government was referring to it as an "incident" or even "alleged incident"

income support

income tax

index plural **indexes**, except for scientific and economic **indices**

indie music, films, etc
Indy short for the Independent, a newspaper

indispensable not indispensible

industrial tribunals have not existed since 1998, when they became **employment tribunals**; they still appear in the pages of the paper with embarrassing frequency despite regular entreaties from the readers' editor in his corrections and clarifications column

infer/imply to infer is to deduce something from evidence; to imply is to hint at something (and wait for someone to infer it)

infinite without limit; does not mean very large

infinitives, split *see split infinitives*

inflammable means the same as **flammable**; the negative is **non-flammable**

initials no spaces or points, whether businesses or individuals, eg WH Smith, PCR Tufnell

Inland Revenue the Revenue on second reference

inner city noun two words, adjective hyphen: inner-city blues made Marvin Gaye wanna holler

innocuous

innuendo plural **innuendoes**

inoculate not innoculate

inquiry not enquiry

inshallah means "God willing" in Arabic

insignia are plural

insisted overused, especially in political stories; just use said

install, instalment

instil, instilled, instilling followed by into

Institute for Fiscal Studies not Institute of Fiscal Studies

insure against risk **assure** life **ensure** make certain

insurgents, insurgency *see terrorism, terrorists*

International Atomic Energy Agency not "authority", its director general is Mohamed ElBaradei

international date line

internet net, web, world wide web, website, chatroom, homepage all lc

Interpol

intifada

introducing people
Never use the following construction to introduce a speaker or a subject: "School standards minister David Miliband said … "

Instead, use the definite article and commas to separate the job from the name, like this: "The school standards minister, David Miliband, said … " (there is only one person with this specific post).

Commas are not used if the description is more general and could apply to more than one person, like this: "The education minister David Miliband said … " (there are several education ministers); or like this: "The former school standards minister Estelle Morris said … " (there have been several).

Another example: "Jonathan Glancey, the Guardian's architecture critic, gave his verdict … " is correct; "The architecture critic Jonathan Glancey gave his verdict … " is fine as well.

We get this wrong somewhere in the paper every day, and we shouldn't

into but **on to**

Inuit not Eskimos, an individual is an **Inuk**

'I don't want to talk grammar. I want to talk like a lady in a flower shop'

(Eliza Doolittle)

George Bernard Shaw
Pygmalion

invalid means not valid or of no worth; do not use to refer to disabled or ill people

invariable, invariably unchanging; often used wrongly to mean hardly ever changing

Iraqi placenames
Use these spellings for Iraq's biggest cities and towns: Amara, Baiji, Baghdad, Baquba, Basra, Diwaniya, Dohuk, Falluja, Haditha, Hilla, Irbil, Kerbala, Kirkuk, Kut, Mosul, Najaf, Nassiriya, Ramadi, Rutba, Samarra, Samawa, Sulaimaniya, Tikrit (note that these transliterations do away with al- prefixes and the final h)

Ireland, Irish Republic not Eire

Irish Travellers uc, recognised as a distinct ethnic group under race relations legislation

iron curtain

ironfounder, ironmonger, ironworks

ironically Avoid when what you mean is strangely, coincidentally, paradoxically or amusingly (if you mean them say so, or leave it up to the reader to decide). There are times when ironically is right but too often it is misused. As

Kingsley Amis put it: "The slightest and most banal coincidence or point of resemblance, or even just-perceptible absence of one, unworthy of a single grunt of interest, gets called 'ironical'." The idiotic "post-ironic", which Amis would be glad he did not live to see, is banned

Isa individual savings account, but no need to spell it out

-ise
not -ize at end of word, eg maximise, synthesise (exception: capsize)

Islam (means "submission to the will of God"). Muslims should never be referred to as "Mohammedans", as 19th-century writers did. It causes serious offence because they insist that they worship God, not the prophet Muhammad.
    "Allah" is simply Arabic for "the God". Both words refer to the

same concept: there is no major difference between God in the Old Testament and Allah in Islam. Therefore it makes sense to talk about "God" in an Islamic context and to use "Allah" in quotations or for literary effect.

The holy book of Islam is the **Qur'an** (not Koran)

Islamist an advocate or supporter of Islamic fundamentalism; the likes of Osama bin Laden and his followers should be described as Islamist terrorists and never as Islamic terrorists

Islamophobia

italics
Use roman for titles of books, films etc; the only exception is the Review, which by special dispensation is allowed to ignore the generally sound advice of George Bernard Shaw: "1 I was reading The Merchant of Venice. 2 I was reading 'The Merchant of Venice'. 3 I was reading *The Merchant of Venice*. The man who cannot see that No 1 is the best looking, as well as the sufficient and sensible form, should print or write nothing but advertisements for lost dogs or ironmongers' catalogues: literature is not for him to meddle with"

ITV1, ITV2

Ivory Coast not "the Ivory Coast" or Côte D'Ivoire; its nationals are **Ivorians**

ivy league universities
Brown, Columbia, Cornell, Dartmouth College, Harvard, Princeton, University of Pennsylvania, Yale

J joules **kJ** kilojoules

Jacuzzi TM, named after its US inventors, Roy and Candido Jacuzzi; call it a whirlpool bath or spa bath unless you're sure it really is a Jacuzzi

jail not gaol

al-Jazeera

jejune naive, unsophisticated (not necessarily anything to do with being young)

jellaba loose cloak with a hood, worn especially in north Africa and the Middle East

Jérez

jerry-builder

jewellery

jib triangular sail or arm of a crane; "I don't like the cut of his jib" means you don't like the look or manner of someone

jibe (not gibe) taunt

jihad used by Muslims to describe three different kinds of struggle: an individual's internal struggle to live out the Muslim faith as well as possible; the struggle to build a good Muslim society; and the struggle to defend Islam, with force if necessary (holy war)

Jobcentre Plus government agency that runs **jobcentres**

jobseeker's allowance

job titles are all lc, editor of the Guardian, governor of the Bank of England, prime minister, etc

jodhpurs

Joe Public, John Doe

John O'Groats

Johns Hopkins University not John Hopkins (one of our most frequent errors)

Johnson Matthey plc metal specialist, not to be confused with **Johnson Matthey Bank**

jokey not joky

Joneses as in "keeping up with the Joneses"; also note "the Joneses' house" (not the Jones' house)

Jonsson, Ulrika

judgment

jumbo jet Boeing 747

junior abbreviate to **Jr** not Jun or Jnr, eg Sammy Davis Jr

just deserts not just desserts, unless you are saying you only want pudding

Ka'bah cube-shaped shrine in the centre of the great mosque in Mecca towards which all Muslims face in prayer; the shrine is not worshipped but used as the focal point of the worship of God

kapok

Kashmir adjective **Kashmiri**; but **cashmere** fabric

Kathmandu capital of Nepal

Kazakhstan adjective **Kazakh**

Kefalonia not Cephalonia

key a useful headline word cheapened by tedious overuse

keyring

K-For Nato peacekeeping force in Kosovo

khaki

Khachaturian, Aram (1903-78) Armenian composer

Khrushchev, Nikita (1894-1971) Soviet leader

kibbutz plural **kibbutzim**

kibosh

kick-off

kilogram/s, kilojoule/s, kilometre/s, kilowatt/s abbreviate as **kg, kJ, km, kW**

King Edward potatoes

King's College, Cambridge comma

King's College London no comma

King's Cross

King's Lynn

King's Road (Chelsea) not "the King's Road"

Kirkcaldy not Kirkaldy; a town in **Fife**, not Fyfe

kissogram

Kitemark TM

knockout

knots measure of nautical miles an hour; do not say "knots per hour"

Knowles, Beyoncé

Korean names like Hong Kong and Taiwanese names, Korean names are written in two parts with a hyphen, eg Kim Jong-il, Kim Dae-jung

Kosovo, Kosovans adjective **Kosovan**, not Kosovar

kowtow

krugerrands

kukri Gurkha knife

Kyrgyzstan adjective **Kyrgyz**

Kyrie Eleison

laager South African encampment **lager** beer

bin Laden, Osama Bin Laden on second reference. Note: Bin Laden has been stripped of his Saudi citizenship, so should be described as Saudi-born but not as a Saudi. His organisation is known as al-Qaida ("the Base")

Lady Blackstone, Lady Jay, Lady Thatcher, etc, not Baroness even on first mention

Lady Macbeth of Mtsensk Shostakovich opera, traditionally misspelt in the Guardian as Mtensk, with occasional variations such as Mtsenk

Lailat al-Miraj Islamic holy day

Lailat al-Qadr Islamic holy day, time for study and prayer

laissez-faire not italicised

Lake District or **the Lakes**

lambast

lamb's wool

lamp-post

lance corporal

Land state of Federal German Republic; use state, eg Hesse, the German state

landmine

Land Registry government department that registers title to land in England and Wales

Land Rover

lang, kd Canadian singer

largesse

La's, the defunct Liverpool rock band; keep apostrophe (abbreviation for Lads)

lasso plural **lassoes**

last post

later often redundant as context will inform the reader: "They will meet this month" rather than "They will meet later this month"

Latin
Some people object to, say, the use of "decimate" to mean destroy on the grounds that in ancient Rome it meant to kill every 10th man; some of them are also likely to complain about so-called split infinitives, a prejudice that goes back to 19th-century Latin teachers who argued that as you can't split infinitives in Latin (they are one word) you shouldn't separate "to" from the verb in English. Others might even get upset about our alleged misuse of grammatical "case" (including cases such as dative and genitive that no longer exist in English).

As the Guardian is written in English, rather than Latin, do not worry about any of this even slightly

latitude like this: 21 deg 14 min S

law lords may be female: we don't say "law ladies"

lawsuit

layby plural **laybys**

lay off does not mean to sack or make redundant, but to send workers home on part pay because of a temporary lack of demand for their product

lbw (cricket)

leap year

learned not learnt, unless you are writing old-fashioned poetry (he learned his tables, a message well learned)

left wing, the left, leftwinger nouns **leftwing** adjective; **hard left, old left**

'Away with him! Away with him! He speaks Latin'
Shakespeare Henry VI Part 2

Legal Aid Board

legal terms
in camera is now known as **in secret** and in chambers **in private**; a writ is a **claim form** and a plaintiff a **claimant**; leave to appeal is **permission to appeal**.

Since the Children Act 1989, access has been known as **contact** and custody is known as **residence**; do not use the older terms

legionnaires' disease
named after an outbreak at a conference of American Legionnaires

lepers do not use: these days the term is regarded as inappropriate and stigmatising; prefer people affected by or people with leprosy

lese-majeste

less/fewer less means smaller in quantity, eg less money; fewer means smaller in number, eg fewer coins

letdown, let-up nouns
let down, let up verbs

leukaemia

level crossing

liaison

libretto plural **librettos**

licence noun **license** verb

lied plural **lieder**

Liège but adjective **Liégeois**

lieutenant colonel, lieutenant general abbreviate on second mention to Col or Gen: Lieutenant Colonel Christopher Mackay, subsequently Col Mackay, etc

lifelong

lightbulb

light year a measure of distance, not time

likable not likeable

like/as if never use the former to mean the latter: "it looks as if he's finished" not "it looks like he's finished"

like/such as like excludes; such as includes: "Cities like Manchester are wonderful" suggests the writer has in mind, say, Sheffield or Birmingham; she actually means "cities such as Manchester".

Do not just automatically change "like" to "such as" —

the following appeared in the paper: "He is not a celebrity, such as Jesse Ventura, the former wrestler…"

likely he is likely to win or he will very likely win, not "he will likely win" — if you want to use that form, say "he will probably win"

lilliputian

limpid means clear or transparent, not limp

linchpin not lynchpin

lineup, lineout

liquefy not liquify

listed buildings
In England and Wales, Grade I-listed (note cap G, roman numeral I) buildings are of exceptional interest; Grade II* are particularly important buildings of more than special interest; Grade II are of special interest, warranting every effort to preserve them. In Scotland and Northern Ireland these categories are replaced by the more logical Grade A, Grade B and Grade C

literally term used, particularly by sports commentators, to denote an event that is not literally true, as in "Manchester City literally came back from the dead"

Lloyd's of London; **names** lc

Lloyds TSB bank

Lord Lloyd-Webber but **Andrew Lloyd Webber**

loan noun; the verb is **lend**

loathe detest
loth unwilling, not loath

lock-in, lockout nouns
lock in, lock out verbs

London assembly elected body of 25 members whose role is to hold the mayor of London to account. Together, assembly and mayor constitute the **Greater London authority** (GLA); note there is no such organisation as the "Greater London assembly"

Londonderry use **Derry** and **Co Derry**

London Eye official name of the millennium wheel

London School of Hygiene and Tropical Medicine

London Transport Users Committee

Long Island iced tea

longitude like this:
149 deg 18 min E

longtime adjective, as in
longtime companion

looking-glass

lord chancellor the
government announced in 2003
that this post would be abolished
and the Lord Chancellor's
Department replaced by the
Department for Constitutional
Affairs

lord chief justice

lord lieutenant no hyphen,
plural **lords lieutenant**

Lords, House of Lords but
the house, not the House; **their
lordships**

Lord's cricket ground

lottery, national lottery but
Lotto and **National Lottery
Commission**

lovable not loveable

lowlife plural **lowlifes**, not
lowlives (for an explanation, see
chapter six of Steven Pinker's
Words and Rules)

loyalists (Northern Ireland)

lumpenproletariat

luvvies a silly cliche; do not use

Luxembourg the country
Luxembourgeois its
inhabitants

luxury, luxurious

Lycra TM; the briefly
fashionable term "lycra louts"
led to complaints from the
Lycra lawyers

lying in state no hyphens

Lynyrd Skynyrd US rock band
(named after a man called
Leonard Skinner)

Lyon not Lyons

Mac or Mc?

Shirley MacLaine, Sue MacGregor, Kelvin MacKenzie, Ewen MacAskill, Murdo MacLeod Sir Trevor McDonald, Malcolm McLaren, David McKie, Gareth McLean Elle Macpherson

mace, the (parliament)
Mace riot control spray

MacDonald, James Ramsay (1866-1937) first Labour prime minister, known as Ramsay MacDonald

McDonald's hamburgers

machiavellian after Nicolo Machiavelli (1469-1527)

machine gun noun
machine-gun verb;
submachine gun

McLuhan, Marshall (1911-80) Canadian author who coined the phrase "the medium is the message"

Macmillan, Harold (1894-1986) Tory prime minister

MacMillan, Kenneth (1929-92) choreographer

MacNeice, Louis (1907-63) Belfast-born poet

madeira wine and cake

madrasa Islamic school

mafia

Mafikeng now spelt thus, though it was Mafeking when it was relieved

magistrates court no apostrophe

maharajah

mailbag, mailvan

mail train

mainland do not use to refer to Great Britain in reports about Northern Ireland

mainmast, mainsail

al-Majid, General Ali Hassan member of Saddam Hussein's revolutionary command council, nicknamed Chemical Ali for his atrocities against Iraq's Kurds (Majid on second reference)

major overused; avoid except in military context

major general abbreviate on second mention to Gen: Major General Ben Summers, subsequently Gen Summers

makeover, makeup no hyphens

Málaga

Malagasy inhabitant or inhabitants of **Madagascar** and the name of their language; the adjective for the country is **Madagascan**

Malaysian names generally the surname comes first, so Mahathir Mohamad becomes Mr Mahathir on second ref. Chinese Malaysian names, like Singaporean names, are in three parts: eg Ling Liong Sik (Mr Ling)

Mall, the

Mamma Mia! musical show featuring Abba songs

mañana

manifesto plural **manifestos**

mankind avoid: use **humankind** or **humanity**

manoeuvre, manoeuvring

Maori singular and plural

Mao Zedong Mao on second mention

marines
Royal Marines, but
US marines

Marks & Spencer at first mention, then **M&S**

marquis not marquess, except where it is the correct formal title, eg Marquess of Blandford

Marrakech

Marseille not Marseilles

marshal (military rank) not marshall, a frequent error; a reader sent in this mnemonic: "Air Chief Marshal Marshall presided at the court martial of the martial arts instructor"

Marshall Aid

Martí, José (1853-95) writer and leader of Cuba's war of independence against Spain

martial law

Mary Celeste not Marie Celeste

massacre the savage killing of large numbers of people, not Stockport County beating Mansfield Town 4-0

massive massively overused; avoid

masterful imperious
masterly skilful

masthead

matinee no accent

matins

matt matt finish, etc

may or might?
The subtle distinctions between these (and between other so-called modal verbs) are gradually disappearing, but they still matter to many of our readers and can be useful.

may implies that the possibility remains open: "The Mies van der Rohe tower may have changed the face of British architecture forever" (it has been built); **might** suggests that the possibility remains open no longer: "The Mies tower might have changed the face of architecture forever" (if only they had built it). Similarly, "they may have played tennis, or they may have gone boating" suggests I don't know what they did; "they might have played tennis if the weather had been dry" means they didn't, because it wasn't.

may also has the meaning of "having permission", so be careful: does "Megawatt Corp may bid for TransElectric Inc" mean that it is considering a bid, or that the competition authorities have allowed it to bid?

May Day May 1 **Mayday** distress signal (from the French "m'aidez!")

mayor of London or anywhere else, lc

MCC, the not "MCC"

meanwhile almost always misused to mean "here's a slight change of subject"

Meat and Livestock Commission

'When I see my name spelt with one word, I want to slap and choke people.

If you do that, you got to be a moron … It's on every poster, every album and every ticket as two words. If you spell it as one, you're an idiot. Bottom line'

Meat Loaf

Meat Loaf sings
meatloaf doesn't

Médecins sans Frontières
international medical aid charity
(don't describe it as French)

Medellín Colombian city

Medical Research Council

media plural of medium: "the
media are sex-obsessed", etc;
but a convention of spiritualists
would be attended by
mediums

medieval not mediaeval

meet, met not meet with, met
with someone

mega horrible; do not use

memento plural **mementoes**

memorandum
plural **memorandums**

menage no accent

menswear

**mental handicap, mentally
handicapped, mentally
retarded** do not use: say
person with learning difficulties

mental health
Take care using language about
mental health issues. In addition
to such clearly offensive and
unacceptable expressions as

loony, maniac, nutter, psycho
and schizo, terms to avoid —
because they stereotype and
stigmatise — include victim of,
suffering from, and afflicted by;
"a person with" is clear, accurate
and preferable to "a person
suffering from". Never use
schizophrenic to mean "in two
minds". And avoid writing "the
mentally ill"— say mentally ill
people, mental health patients or
people with mental health
problems

Messiaen, Olivier (1908-92)
French composer

metaphor traditionally defined
as the application to one thing
of a name belonging to another,
eg bowling blitz, economic
meltdown, "every language is a
temple in which the soul of those
who speak it is enshrined" (Oliver
Wendell Holmes)

Meteorological Office or
Met Office

metres write metres out in full,
to avoid confusion with million
(an obvious exception would be
in an article about athletics, eg
she won the 400m)

metric system
The Guardian uses the metric
system for weights and
measures; exceptions are the

mile and the pint. Since
understanding of the two
systems is a matter of
generations, conversions (in
brackets) to imperial units should
be provided wherever this seems
useful, though usually one
conversion — the first — will
suffice. Imperial units in quoted
matter should be retained, and
converted to metric [in square
brackets] if it doesn't ruin the
flow of the quote.

It is not necessary to convert
moderate distances between
metres and yards, which are
close enough for rough and
ready purposes (though it is
preferable to use metres), or
small domestic quantities: two
litres of wine, a kilogram of sugar,
a couple of pounds of apples, a
few inches of string. Small units
should be converted when
precision is required: 44mm
(1.7in) of rain fell in two hours.
Tons and tonnes (metric) are also
close enough for most purposes

to do without conversion; again use tonnes.

Body weights and heights should always be converted in brackets: metres to feet and inches, kilograms to stones/pounds. Geographical heights and depths, of people, buildings, monuments, etc, should be converted, metres to feet. In square measurement, land is given in sq metres, hectares and sq km, with sq yards, acres or sq miles in brackets where there is space to provide a conversion. The floor areas of buildings are conventionally expressed in sq metres (or sq ft). Take great care in conversions of square and cubic measures

Metropolitan police the Met at second mention; commissioner of the Metropolitan police, Met commissioner is acceptable

mexican wave

Miami Beach US city

mic abbreviation for microphone

mid-90s, mid-60s, etc

mid-Atlantic but **transatlantic**

midday

middle ages

middle America

Middle East never Mid, even in headlines

middle England

Middlesbrough not Middlesborough

Midlands, east Midlands (but **East Midlands airport**), **West Midlands**

midterm no hyphen

midweek

midwest (US)

Milad al-Nabi Islamic festival celebrating the birth of the prophet; many Muslims disapprove of celebrating this event

mileage

Militant tendency

military
For British brigades and divisions use cardinal numbers: 7 Armoured Brigade, 1 UK Armoured Division, 40 Commando, etc; for British battalions and regiments use ordinals, eg 2nd Battalion Royal

Regiment of Fusiliers (for US divisions the style is as follows: 101st Air Assault, 82nd Airborne).

You go **aboard** a ship and when you are **on board** you may be welcomed aboard, but you sail or serve or travel in a ship. Note also that British ships are written "HMS Ark Royal", not "the HMS Ark Royal". When HMS is dropped, mariners shun the definite article, eg "he served in Invincible", though inserting one can avoid ambiguities, eg "he served in the Plymouth" (the ship not the city).

A brief guide to weapons and equipment, etc:

Awacs airborne warning and control system, found on board the E-3 Sentry (a modified Boeing); Awacs is singular
B-52, F-16 note hyphens
ballistic missile has no wings or fins, and follows a ballistic trajectory, eg the Iraqi Scud
cruise missile missile with its own engine, best known is the Tomahawk
Harm high-speed anti-radiation missile, anti-SAM weapon
Istar stands for intelligence, surveillance, target, acquisition and reconnaissance, a "real-time" intelligence gathering system that aims to let decision makers respond to events as they occur

Jdam joint direct attack munition, the satellite-guided smartbomb
Lantirn stands for low altitude navigation and targeting infrared for night, the equipment allows fighters to fly at low altitudes, at night, and under the weather
Moab massive ordnance air blast, nicknamed mother of all bombs
SAMs surface-to-air missiles
Sead suppression of enemy air defences
Tornado plural **Tornados**

A jargon-busting guide to the armed forces' command structure and organisation, ranks, and weapons and equipment follows:

Whitehall

The head of the armed forces is the **chief of the defence staff**, who is the chief military adviser to the defence secretary, equal in status to the permanent secretary of the Ministry of Defence on the civilian side. The rest of the defence staff comprises the vice-chief and the three service chiefs: chief of the naval staff, chief of the general staff, chief of the air staff, and their respective assistant chiefs. They and their various aides, advisers and experts (staff officers) make up the top-level

HQ, at the MoD in Whitehall.

The MoD is divided into 11 sections headed by what it calls TLB (top level budget) holders, five of which are concerned with operations:

1 Chief of Joint Operations, responsible for all military operations, HQ at Northwood, north-west London

2 Navy: Commander in Chief Fleet

3 Army 1: Land Command

4 Army 2: General Officer Commanding, Northern Ireland

5 RAF: Strike Command

Each force has a personnel TLB, the other three are Central, Defence Procurement Agency and Defence Logistics Organisation.

Command structures in all three services are complicated by various joint commands and joint operations, either of two or more services or with other Nato/EU forces.

Royal Navy

The senior service: it was formed first, and its officers are senior to army and RAF officers of equivalent rank. The army, in turn, is senior to the RAF.

Command structure and organisation

Head: first sea lord and chief of the naval staff

Top body: the Admiralty Board, chaired by the defence secretary

Operational body: Navy Board, headed by first sea lord (1SL) and including commander in chief fleet, and second sea lord (deals with personnel, etc) and others

Work gets done by Battle Fleet Staff, headed by CinCFleet, who is a full admiral, with HQs in Portsmouth and Plymouth

Ships

Three aircraft carriers: they carry helicopters crewed by the Fleet Air Arm and Harrier jets crewed by a joint FAA and RAF command, and a Royal Marine commando unit. In a taskforce or other assembly of ships the carrier will have the admiral (or commodore) commanding on board, and will fly his flag, hence it is the flagship

Amphibious assault ships: land marines, etc, directly on land or by helicopter; like a small aircraft carrier

Destroyers and frigates: armed mainly with missiles and helicopters, for attack and defence against aircraft and other ships

Mine countermeasure vessels (MCMVs)

Assorted hydrographic survey ships, fisheries protection, patrol boats, etc

Submarine Service: ballistic missile subs (SSBN) are nuclear armed; fleet subs (SSN) are nuclear powered.

Training establishments on shore, including RN Reserve and University Royal Navy Units, are labelled HMS. The main bases (Portsmouth, Devonport, Clyde) are HMNB; Fleet Air Arm airfields are RNAS (royal naval air station) but also have a ship name, eg RNAS Yeovilton is also HMS Heron; NROs (naval regional offices/officers) are the regional flag wavers, each of four headed by a commodore.

Fleet Air Arm: organised in naval air squadrons, flying Merlin, Lynx and Sea King helicopters and Sea Harrier jump jets; its ranks are navy style.

Royal Fleet Auxiliary: tankers, supply, landing and repair ships; commanding officer is Commodore RFA, answering to CinCFleet, crews are civilian ships are RFA (not HMS) Sir Galahad, etc.

Royal Marines are soldiers in ships (and planes), part of the navy but they have army-style ranks, eg colonel, major, sergeant. The main operational force is 3 Commando, which comprises three commando units, supported by Royal Engineers and Royal Artillery (army) commando units. Their

main base and training centre is RM Poole. A branch of the Royal Marines is the **SBS** (Special Boat Service) whose fighters are special forces.

Ranks
Officers:

Admiral of the Fleet; Admiral (abbreviated to Adm on subsequent mentions); Vice Admiral (Adm); Rear Admiral (Adm). All four are flag officers, entitled to fly their flag in the ship (flagship) in which they are quartered. The captain of such a ship is a flag captain. A flag lieutenant is an admiral's aide-de-camp. Confusingly, the navy is liable to refer to/address any of these as flag for short

Commodore: likely to command, for example, a small force of ships or shore station (the title is also given to the chief captain of a shipping line)

Captain (abbreviated to Capt); Commander (Cmdr); Lieutenant Commander (Lt Cmdr); Lieutenant (Lt); Sub-Lieutenant (Sub Lt); Midshipman. The captain of a small ship will not have the rank of captain.

Ratings:
Warrant Officer (WO); Chief Petty Officer (CPO); Petty Officer (PO); leading and able ratings are usually addressed according to

their trade or field of expertise, eg Leading Artificer (a naval term for engineer), Able Communications Technician, etc.

Weapons

Spearfish torpedo: wire and sonar-guided, homes on its target

Stingray torpedo: light, aircraft- or ship-borne

Paams: principal anti-air missile system, on destroyers, Aster 15 and Aster 30 (longer range) missiles

Sea Wolf (on frigates) and Sea Dart (destroyers): defensive anti-air missiles

Harpoon (frigate): anti-ship missile

Tomahawk (submarines): land attack cruise missile, 1,000-mile range

Goalkeeper: close range (up to 1,500 metres) defensive weapon system with seven-barrel Gatling gun firing at the rate of 70 rounds a second

Phalanx: last-chance 20mm Gatling gun, 3,000 rpm

114mm/4.5in Mk8 gun: the only real gun left in the navy, 21kg shell, 25 rpm, fitted to all frigates and destroyers

British army

Command structure and organisation

Head: chief of the general staff

Top body: the Army Board, chaired by the defence secretary

Main HQ is Joint Permanent Headquarters, Northwood (joint with the other services)

HQ Land Command, at Erskine barracks, Wilton, near Salisbury, commands fighting soldiers at home and abroad, and addition there are:

HQ General Officer Commanding, Northern Ireland

plus HQ British Forces Cyprus, HQ British Forces Falkland Islands

The next level of command is the division. There are two operationally ready divisions, 1 (UK) Armoured Division, which is confusingly based in Germany, attached to Nato Allied Rapid Reaction Corps, and 3 (UK) Division, HQ Bulford, Wiltshire, part of the Nato Allied Rapid Reaction Corps. Numbers 2, 4 and 5 are administrative organisations, geographically based in Britain, capable of being bumped up if need be.

The next level is the brigade, historically consisting of three battalions/regiments of infantry or armour or artillery and support troops, but these days most units at most levels are mixed bunches. Of particular interest is 16 Air Assault Brigade, the newest and biggest (6,000) with a joint army/RAF HQ at Colchester; it is the primary rapid reaction force, including two Parachute Regiment battalions, one line infantry battalion, RAF and Army Air Corps units, artillery, engineers and other support services.

Corps are the professional organisations, both fighting and support. The infantry is technically a corps, though not often referred to as such, and there are the Royal Armoured Corps, Royal Corps of Logistics, etc.

Infantry

section: eight to 12 soldiers commanded by an NCO (corporal)
platoon: 25-40 soldiers commanded by a lieutenant, aided by a sergeant
company: three platoons and a HQ, 150 officers and men commanded by a major
battalion/regiment: three companies, a support company and a HQ company, 500-800 soldiers commanded by a lieutenant colonel, assisted by an adjutant (usually a major). Some regiments have several battalions, ie 1, 2 and 3 Para. During the first and second world wars each regiment had many

battalions. Many regiments have been disbanded: some amalgamated with others; some historical regimental names are preserved at company level (*see armoured division*)

The **SAS** is a regiment and counts as part of the infantry, but it is also designated special forces.

Armoured units

troop: four tanks, 12 troopers, commanded by a first or second lieutenant, a sergeant and two corporals, each of whom commands a tank
squadron: 14 tanks, commanded by a major (but there are reconnaissance squadrons with light armoured cars, etc)
regiment: 58 tanks, about 550 officers and troopers, commanded by a lieutenant colonel
brigade: three to four battalions/regiments grouped together with added support troops, commanded by a brigadier (in historical terms a brigade would be three infantry battalions but most of them are now made up of a wide range of fighting and support units of various sizes)
division: two to four brigades grouped together with added support troops, 16,000-30,000 soldiers commanded by a major

general (30,000 may be theoretical, but the biggest is about 18,000, and others are as low as a couple of thousand). In addition, regiments are grouped in divisions, viz Guards Division, Scottish Division, Queen's Division, etc, and the Brigade of Gurkhas (which includes the Royal Irish regiment)

The Armoured Division includes the various remaining mounted units, Life Guards, Blues and Greys, assorted Hussars, Dragoons, Lancers, etc, retained for ceremonial purposes when the cavalry regiments were turned into tank regiments and gradually lost their individual identity.

Support troops are drawn from:

The Royal Regiment of Artillery (but it has many regiments, each with its own number, which are historical rather than an indication of the number currently in being). It is divided into batteries, not companies, privates are called gunners, corporals are bombardiers

Royal Engineers (a number of regiments, ie 21 Royal Engineers Regiment, plus battalions of the Royal Electrical and Mechanical Engineers (REME), which also tends to link with Logistics

The various corps, including: Royal Corps of Logistics (transport and supply of ammunition, equipment, food, etc Formerly Transport Corps, formerly Royal Army Service Corps)

Royal Signals
Army Air Corps
Intelligence Corps
Royal Army Medical Corps (plus RA Dental and Veterinary Corps, and Queen Alexandra's Royal Army Nursing Corps)

Adjutant General's Corps (lawyers, administrators, teachers, Provost Branch, including Royal Military Police)

Ranks

Officers:

Field Marshal; General (abbreviated to Gen); Lieutenant General (Gen); Major General (Gen); Brigadier (Brig); Colonel (Col); Lieutenant Colonel (Col); Major (Maj); Captain (Capt); Lieutenant (Lt); Second Lieutenant (Lt).

Non-commissioned officers:

Warrant Officer First Class (WOI) — warrant officers hold their warrant, as commissioned officers hold their commission, from the sovereign; historically they were professional types rather than "gentlemen"; Warrant Officer Second Class (WOII), includes Regimental Quartermaster Sergeant (RQMS); Sergeant (Sgt) (Colour Sergeant, in cavalry/armoured regiments);

Corporal (Cpl)/Bombardier (Bdr); Lance Corporal (L/Cpl) or Lance Bombardier (L/Bdr) in the artillery. Some NCOs have regimental/corps titles other than those indicated.

According to the corps or regiment, the rank of Private (Pte) may be gunner, sapper (engineers), trooper (cavalry, armour), signalman, craftsman, driver, fusilier, ranger, kingsman, rifleman, airtrooper, etc.

Weapons and equipment

Light arms from the SA80 family — L85 individual weapon and L86 light support weapon — replace old-fashioned rifles and light machine guns; heavy machine gun; general purpose machine gun; light machine gun; Milan anti-tank weapon; 51mm and 81mm mortars; light anti-armour weapon (sits on the shoulder, looks like a bazooka); sniper rifles.

Armour: Challenger 2 battletank; Warrior infantry fighting vehicle; Saxon armoured personnel carrier; Sabre armoured light recce vehicle; various others, eg Samaritan armoured ambulance, Samson armoured recovery vehicle (note that tanks, armoured personnel carriers and self-propelled guns look similar but have different

roles. A tank's main role is to attack other tanks and armour. An armoured personnel carrier carries infantry, commanders, signallers or other support troops. Spata — stands for self-propelled artillery-tracked artillery — are big guns with their own engines).

Artillery: multiple launch rocket system; AS90 self-propelled gun (looks similar to a tank, but tanks are primarily used on the move against other armour); L118 light gun; Starstreak high-velocity missile.

Aircraft: Apache attack; Bell 212; Gazelle and Lynx helicopters; Britten-Norman Islander plane.

Royal Air Force

Command structure and organisation

Head: chief of the air staff, senior to commander in chief strike command and deputy CinC strike command

Strike Command HQ at RAF High Wycombe, with three groups:
1 all strike aircraft
2 all support aircraft
3 Joint Force Harrier, mix of RAF and navy, commanded by a naval officer;

UK Combined Air Operations Centre at High Wycombe works with RAF, RN and Nato forces to scramble the jets if the missiles start coming in.

The basic units are squadrons, those at the sharp end being strike/attack and offensive support; air defence and airborne early warning, and reconnaissance. HQs, airfields and other establishments are RAF stations, eg RAF Boulmer.

Ranks

Officers: Marshal of the Royal Air Force; Air Chief Marshal; Air Marshal; Air Vice-Marshal; Air Commodore (equivalent to navy commodore and army brigadier); Group Captain (Group Capt, equivalent to captain, colonel); Wing Commander (Wing Cdr, = commander, lieutenant colonel); Squadron Leader (Sqn Ldr, – lieutenant commander, major); Flight Lieutenant (Flt Lt, = lieutenant, captain; Flying Officer, (= sub-lieutenant, lieutenant); Pilot Officer (Plt Off, = midshipman, second lieutenant — except that midshipmen are junior to their army and air force counterparts).

Other ranks:
Master Aircrew (= warrant officer, WOI); Warrant Officer (WO, = warrant officer, WOI); Flight

Sergeant (FS, = chief petty officer, staff corporal, staff sergeant); Chief Technician (Ch Tech, = chief petty officer, staff corporal, staff sergeant); Sergeant (Sgt, = petty officer, sergeant, corporal of horse); Corporal (Cpl, = leading rate, corporal, bombardier); Junior Technician (Jr Tech, = able or ordinary rate, private or its equivalents, as are the remaining ranks); Senior Aircraftman/Aircraftwoman and Leading Aircraftman/Aircraftwoman.

Equipment
Offensive aircraft:

Harrier single-seat attack, vertical takeoff and landing, general purpose bomb, cluster bombs, laser-guided bombs, anti-tank bombs

Jaguar single-seat attack and recce, general purpose bomb, cluster bombs, guided bomb, rockets, cannon, defensive air-to-air missiles

Tornado GR4 twin seat, swing wing, supersonic, guided bombs, cruise missiles

Typhoon (Eurofighter) upcoming replacement for Jaguar and Tornado F3, bristling with all the above weapons

Defensive aircraft:
Sentry ex-Boeing 707, flying radar station

Tornado F3 two-seater supersonic, air-to-air and anti-radar missiles

Recce/marine patrol:

Canberra 1940s bomber, now high-altitude recce

Nimrod based on Comet, the first jetliner

Transport:

Globemaster, Hercules, Tristar, VC10

Weapons

air-to-air missiles: Asraam, Aim-9 Sidewinder, Amraam, Skyflash

anti-shipping: Harpoon, Stingray

short-range air-to-surface (gp bombs): CVR-7 1,000lb bomb, Paveway II and III, Enhanced Paveway (guided gp bombs), Maverick (missile)

long-range air-launched missiles: Alarm, Brimstone, Storm Shadow

surface-to-air (defensive) missile system: Rapier

cannon: Aden 30mm/1,200-1,400 rounds a minute (the rate of fire, the ammo box carries only 150 rounds); Mauser 27mm, 1,000/1,700 rounds a minute rate of fire

Finally, here is our style for US aircraft which played a big part in the wars in Iraq and Afghanistan:

F-14 Tomcat, F-15 Eagle, F-16 Fighting Falcon, F/A-18 Hornet/Super Hornet, F-117 Nighthawk stealth fighter, B-52 Stratofortress, B-2 stealth bomber, B-1B Lancer

militate/mitigate to militate against something is to influence it (his record militated against his early release); to mitigate means to lessen an offence (in mitigation, her counsel argued that she came from a broken home)

millenary, millennium, millennia

Millennium Dome at first mention, then just **the dome**

millennium wheel its official name is **London Eye**

million in copy use **m** for sums of money, units or inanimate objects: £10m, 45m tonnes of coal, 30m doses of vaccine; but **million** for people or animals: 1 million people, 23 million rabbits, etc; use **m** in headlines

mimic, mimicked, mimicking

min contraction of minute/minutes, no full point

mineworker

minibus, minicab, miniskirt, minivan

minimum plural **minima**

ministers

minuscule not miniscule

mistakable, unmistakable

misuse, misused no hyphen

MLA member of the Northern Ireland assembly, eg Bairbre de Brun MLA (stands for member of the legislative assembly)

MLitt master of letters, not master of literature

Moby-Dick Herman Melville's classic is, believe it or not, hyphenated

Modern in the sense of Modern British, to distinguish it from "modern art"

Moët & Chandon

Mönchengladbach

moneyed not monied
moneys not monies

Mongol one of the peoples of Mongolia

Monk, Thelonious (1920-82) American jazz pianist and composer, generally but erroneously referred to in the Guardian and elsewhere as "Thelonius"

Montenegro inhabited by **Montenegrins**

Moors murders committed in the 1960s by Ian Brady and Myra Hindley

more than generally preferable to over: there were more than 20,000 people at the game, it will cost more than £100 to get it fixed; but she is over 18

Morissette, Alanis

morning-after pill

morris dance

Morrisons for the stores, Wm Morrison Supermarkets is the name of the company

mortgage borrower, lender the person borrowing the money is the mortgagor, the lender is both the mortgagee and the mortgage holder; to avoid confusion, call the mortgagor the mortgage borrower and the mortgagee the mortgage lender

mosquito plural **mosquitoes**

mother of parliaments
the great Liberal politician and
Manchester Guardian reader
John Bright described England,
the country (not Westminster, the
institution), as the mother of
parliaments

mother of three, etc, not
mother-of-three

motorcar, motorcycle

Motörhead

motorways write M1, not
M1 motorway

mottoes

movable

mph no points

MPs

Mr, Ms, Mrs, Miss use after
first mention on news (but not
sport) pages and in leading
articles, unless you are writing
about an artist, author, journalist,
musician, criminal or dead
person; defendants keep their
honorifics unless they are
convicted

Mrs, Miss or Ms? we use
whichever the woman in
question prefers: with most
women in public life (Mrs May,

Miss Widdecombe) that
preference is well known; if you
don't know, try to find out; if
that proves impossible, use Ms

MSP member of the Scottish
parliament, eg Sir David Steel
MSP

Muhammad
Muslims consider Muhammad to
be the last of God's prophets,
who delivered God's final
message. They recognise Moses
and Jesus as prophets also.
   The above transliteration is our
style for the prophet's name and
for most Muhammads living in
Arab countries, though where
someone's preferred spelling is
known we respect it, eg
Mohamed Al Fayed, Mohamed
ElBaradei. The spelling
Mohammed (or variants) is
considered archaic by most
British Muslims today, and
disrespectful by many of them

Muhammad Ali

mujahideen collective noun
for people fighting a jihad; the
singular is **mujahid**

mukhabarat Saddam
Hussein's secret police

**multicultural, multimedia,
multimillion** but
multi-ethnic

Mumbai (formerly Bombay)
use this phrase at first mention

Murphy's law "If there are two
or more ways to do something,
and one of those ways can result
in a catastrophe, then someone
will do it"; also known as sod's
law

museums initial caps, eg
British Museum, Natural History
Museum, Victoria and Albert
Museum (V&A on second
reference), Metropolitan Museum
of Art, etc

Muslim not Moslem

Muzak TM

MW megawatts **mW** milliwatts

Getting it wrong:
our most common mistakes

Even senior Guardian journalists get confused over homophones
(words that sound the same but are spelt differently), particularly
these:

defuse (render harmless), **diffuse** (spread about)

incidence (amount, eg a high incidence of mistakes),
incidents (events)

phased (in stages), **fazed** (overwhelmed)

grizzly (bear), **grisly** (gruesome)

balk (stop short, obstruct), **baulk** (part of a snooker table)

We also get confused over these:

prevaricate means "to speak or act falsely with intent to
deceive" but we sometimes use it when we mean to say
procrastinate, to put off until tomorrow

overestimate often comes out as **underestimate**,
which means the opposite

ancestors is written where **descendants** is meant
surprisingly often

'I know of only one rule:
style cannot be too clear,
too simple'

Stendhal

And placenames get mixed up or misspelt:

Colombia is the country, often misspelt as "Columbia" as in **District of Columbia** or **Columbia University**, both in the US

On the subject of American colleges, **Johns Hopkins University** in Baltimore appears far too often as "John Hopkins University" which does not exist; we also call **Stanford University** "Stamford" with depressing frequency

Middlesbrough is in **Teesside**, but you will often read that "Middlesborough" is in "Teeside"

Similarly, **Kirkcaldy**, **Fife** is not "Kirkaldy, Fyfe"

Other common spelling mistakes

linchpin is often misspelt as "lynchpin"

de rigueur ("de rigeur")

fluoride ("flouride")

minuscule ("miniscule")

supersede ("supercede")

seize ("sieze")

siege ("seige")

targeted, targeting ("targetted, targetting")

Nabokov, Vladimir (1899-1977) Russian-born author of Lolita; not Nabakov

nailbomb

naive, naively, naivety

names
Avoid the "chancellor Gordon Brown" syndrome: do not use constructions, beloved of the tabloids, such as "chancellor Gordon Brown said". The chancellor refers to his job, not his title. Prominent figures can just be named, with their function at second mention: "Gordon Brown said last night" (first mention); "the chancellor said" (subsequent mentions).

Where it is thought necessary to explain who someone is, write "Neil Warnock, the Sheffield United manager, said" or "the Sheffield United manager, Neil Warnock, said". In such cases the commas around the name indicate there is only one person in the position, so write "the Tory leader, Michael Howard, said" (only one person in the job), but "the former Tory prime minister John Major said" (there have been many)

Nasa National Aeronautics and Space Administration, but no need to spell out

nation do not use when you mean country or state; reserve nation to describe people united by language, culture and history so as to form a distinct group within a larger territory. And beware of attributing the actions of a government or a military force to a national population (eg, "The Israelis have killed 400 children during the intifada"). Official actions always have opponents within a population; if we don't acknowledge this, we oversimplify the situation and shortchange the opponents

National Association of Schoolmasters Union of Women Teachers (NASUWT); we are stuck with these initials unless the organisation changes its name to something more sensible; call it "the union" after first mention

National Audit Office

National Grid owner and operator of the British electricity transmission system since the industry was privatised in 1990

national insurance

nationalists (Northern Ireland)

national lottery

National Offender Management Service

National Savings the former Post Office Savings Bank, now a government agency (full name National Savings and Investments)

Native Americans Geronimo was a Native American (not an American Indian or Red Indian); George Bush is a native American

Nato North Atlantic Treaty Organisation, but no need to spell out

naught nothing
nought the figure 0

Navarro-Valls, Dr Joaquín Vatican spokesman

navy but **Royal Navy**

Nazi but **nazism**

nearby one word, whether adjective or adverb: the pub nearby; the nearby pub

nearsighted, nearsightedness

neophilia even if you have always wanted to appear in Private Eye, resist the temptation to write such nonsense as "grey is the new black", "billiards is the new snooker", "Umbria is the new Tuscany", etc

nerve-racking

Nestlé

Netherlands, the not Holland, which is only part of the country; use Dutch as the adjective. Exception: the Dutch football team is generally known as Holland

nevertheless but **none the less**

new, now often redundant

Newcastle-under-Lyme hyphens **Newcastle upon Tyne** no hyphens

New Labour but **old Labour**

news agency

newsagent, newsprint, newsreel

newspaper titles the Guardian, the New York Times, etc; no need to coyly add "newspaper" to the Sun, the Daily Sport, etc, as if our readers had never heard of them

New Testament

new year lc, but **New Year's Day, New Year's Eve**

New York City but **New York state**

next of kin

NHS national health service, but not necessary to spell out; health service is also OK

Nichpa National Infection Control and Health Protection Agency

Nietzsche, Friedrich Wilhelm (1844-1900) German philosopher

Nigerian names Surnames do not exist in the north of Nigeria: a typical name would be Isa Sani Sokoto (Isa the son of Sani who comes from the town of Sokoto); so best to write in full

nightcap, nightdress, nightfall, nightgown, nightshade, nightshirt

Nobel prize Nobel peace prize, Nobel prize for literature, etc

No 1 in the charts, the world tennis No 1, etc — with thin (non-breaking) space before the number

No 10 (Downing Street) — with thin space before the 10

no plural **noes**

no-brainer means something along the lines of "this is so obvious, you don't need a brain to know it" not "only someone with no brain would think this"

no campaign, yes campaign not No campaign, "no" campaign or any of the other variants

no man's land no hyphens

no one not no-one

noncommissioned officer

nonconformist

none It is a (very persistent) myth that "none" has to take a singular verb, but plural is acceptable and often sounds more natural, eg "none of the current squad are good enough to play in the Premiership", "none of the issues have been resolved"

none the less but **nevertheless**

north north London, north-east England, the north-west, etc

north of the border avoid this expression: the Guardian is a national newspaper

northern hemisphere

north pole

North-West Frontier Province Pakistan

North York Moors national park; but **North Yorkshire Moors** railway

nosy not nosey

noticeboard

notebook, notepaper

Nottingham Forest, Notts County

Notting Hill carnival

numbers Spell out from one to nine; integers from 10 to 999,999; thereafter use m or bn for sums of money, quantities or inanimate objects in copy, eg £10m, 5bn tonnes of coal, 30m doses of vaccine; but million or billion for people or animals, eg 1 million people, 3 billion rabbits, etc; in headlines use m or bn

numeracy
Numbers have always contained power, and many a journalist will tremble at the very sight of them. But most often the only maths we need to make sense of them is simple arithmetic. Far more important are our critical faculties, all too often switched off at the first sniff of a figure.

It's easy to be hoodwinked by big numbers in particular. But are they really so big? Compared with what? And what is being assumed? A government announcement of an extra £X million a year will look far less impressive if divided by 60 million (the British population) and/or 52 (weeks in the year). That's quite apart from the fact that it was probably trumpeted last week already, as part of another, bigger number. We have to be aggressive when interpreting the spin thrown at us.

The legal profession has, in the same way, been forced to put DNA evidence in the dock. If the probability of the accused and the culprit sharing the same genetic profile is one in 3 million, then there are 19 other people in Britain alone who share the same DNA "match".

Never invent a big figure when a small one will do. Totting jail sentences together ("the six men were jailed for a total of 87 years") is meaningless as well as irritating. Similarly, saying that something has an area the size of 150 football pitches, or is

"eight times the size of Wales", is cliched and may not be helpful.

Here is an easy three-point guide to sidestepping common "mythematics" traps:

1 Be careful in conversions, don't muddle metric and imperial, or linear, square and cubic measures. Square miles and miles square are constantly confused: an area 10 miles square is 10 miles by 10 miles, which equals 100 square miles.

2 Be extremely wary of converting changes in temperature; you run the risk of confusing absolute and relative temperatures, eg while a temperature of 2C is about the same as 36F, a temperature change of 2C corresponds to a change of 3.6F (each degree of increase in celsius is 1.8 in fahrenheit)

3 If calculating percentages, beware the "rose by/fell by X%" construction: an increase from 3% to 5% is a 2 percentage point increase or a 2-point increase, not a 2% increase

Nuremberg

OAPs, old age pensioners
do not use: they are
pensioners or **old people**;
note also that we should take
care using the word elderly — it
should not be used to describe
anyone younger than 70

obbligato not obligato

O'Brian, Patrick author of
Master and Commander

obscenities *see swearwords*

obtuse "mentally slow or
emotionally insensitive" (Collins);
often confused with **abstruse**
(hard to understand) or **obscure**

occupied territories

oceans, seas uc, eg Atlantic
Ocean, Red Sea

Ofcom Office of Communications,
the broadcasting and
telecommunications regulator

offhand, offside
but **off-licence**

**Office for National
Statistics**

Office of Fair Trading
OFT on second mention

**Office of the Deputy Prime
Minister** avoid the ugly
abbreviation ODPM after first
mention by calling it Mr
Prescott's office, the office,
the department, etc

Oh! not O!

oilfield

oil painting

oil production platform for
production of oil **oil rig** for
exploration and drilling

OK is OK; "okay" is not

Old Testament

O-levels hyphen

Olympic games or just **Olympics**

omelette

ongoing prefer continuous or continual

online

only can be ambiguous if not placed next to the word or phrase modified: "I have only one ambition" is clearer than "I only have one ambition"

on to but **into**

Op 58, No 2 music style

opencast

ophthalmic

opossum

opposition, the

or do not use "or" when explaining or amplifying — rather than "the NUT, or National Union of Teachers" say "The NUT (National Union of Teachers)" or, even better, "The National Union of Teachers" at first mention and then just "the NUT" or "the union"

ordinance direction, decree

Ordnance Survey Britain's national mapping agency ("ordnance" because such work was originally undertaken by the army)

Organisation for Economic Cooperation and Development OECD on second reference

outed, outing take care with these terms: if we say, for example, that a paedophile was outed, we are equating him with a gay person being outed; use exposed or revealed instead

outgrow, outgun, outmanoeuvre, outpatient

outward bound we have been sued twice by the Outward Bound Trust when we have reported that people have died on "outward bound" courses that

'I have found by experience that no one persistently using onto [rather than on to] writes anything much worth reading'

Kingsley Amis

were nothing to do with the trust; use a safer term such as outdoor adventure or adventure training

over not overly *see more than*

overestimate, overstate take care that you don't mean **underestimate** or **understate** (we often get this wrong)

overrule

Oxford comma a comma before the final "and" in lists: straightforward ones (he ate ham, eggs and chips) do not need one, but sometimes it can help the reader (he ate cereal, kippers, bacon, eggs, toast and marmalade, and tea)

oxymoron does not just vaguely mean self-contradictory; an oxymoron is a figure of speech in which apparently contradictory terms are used in conjunction, such as bittersweet, living death, "darkness visible" (Paradise Lost), "the living dead" (The Waste Land); one of Margaret Atwood's characters thought "interesting Canadian" was an oxymoron

pace Latin tag meaning "by the leave of", as a courteous nod to the views of a dissenting author, or "even acknowledging the existence of", not "such as"

Pacific Ocean

paean song of praise
paeon metrical foot of one long and three short syllables

El País

Palestinian Authority becomes "the authority" on second reference

Palme d'Or (Cannes film festival)

Palme, Olof (1927-86) Swedish prime minister who was assassinated in a Stockholm street (not Olaf)

Palmer-Tomkinson, Tara

Pandora's box

panel, panelled, panelling

paparazzo plural **paparazzi;** named after a character in Fellini's 1960 film La Dolce Vita

papier-mache

paralleled

parentheses *see brackets*

Parker Bowles, Camilla no hyphen

Parkinson's disease

Parkinson's law "Work expands so as to fill the time available for its completion"

parliament, parliamentary but cap up those parliaments referred to by their name in the relevant language, eg Knesset, Folketing, Duma, etc

Parthenon marbles official name, recognised by both Britain and Greece, for the Elgin marbles

party lc in name of organisation, eg Labour party

Pashtuns make up about 40% of the Afghan population (called Pathans during the British Raj); singular **Pashtun**; they speak **Pashtu**

passerby plural **passersby**

passive voice strive for active verbs: compare "the mat was sat upon by the cat" with "the cat sat on the mat"

Passport Agency

password

pasteurise

Patent Office

patients are discharged from hospital, not released

payback, payday, payout

peacekeeper, peacetime

Peak District

Pearl Harbor use American English spellings for US placenames

pedaller cyclist **peddler** drug dealer **pedlar** hawker

peers
Avoid writing "Lord Asquith's Liberal government", or "Lady Thatcher took power in 1979"; when talking about people before they were given peerages use their names/titles at the time (eg Herbert Asquith, Mrs Thatcher).

Also avoid the construction "Lady Helena Kennedy": in this case we would write Lady Kennedy or Helena Kennedy, or — if really pushed — Lady (Helena) Kennedy (but never Baroness Kennedy)

peewit

peking duck

pendant adjective **pendent**

peninsula adjective **peninsular**

penknife

pensioners do not call them "old age pensioners" or "OAPs"; take similar care with the word "elderly", which should never be used to describe someone under 70

peony flower

per avoid; use English: "She earns £30,000 a year" is better than "per year". If you must use it, the Latin preposition is followed by another Latin word,

The**Guardian** stylebook

123

eg per capita, not per head.
Exception: miles per hour, which
we write mph

per cent use the % symbol in
headlines and copy

percentage rises probably
our most common lapse into
"mythematics": an increase from
3% to 5% is a 2 percentage
point increase or a 2-point
increase, not a 2% increase; any
sentence saying "such and such
rose or fell by X%" should be
considered and checked carefully

Pérez de Cuéllar, Javier
Peruvian diplomat and former UN
secretary general (Mr Pérez de
Cuéllar on second mention)

Performing Right Society
not Rights

permissible

Peronists supporters of the
nationalist/populist ideology of
the late Argentinian president
Juan Domingo Perón

personal equity plan Pep

persons No! They are people
(can you imagine Barbra
Streisand singing "Persons who
need persons"?)

Perspex TM

peshmerga Kurdish opposition
fighters

phenomenon
plural **phenomena**

Philippines inhabited by
Filipinos (male) and **Filipinas**
(female); adjective **Filipino** for
both sexes, but **Philippine** for,
say, a Philippine island or the
Philippine president

Philips electronics company
Phillips screwdriver, auction
house

philistine

Phnom Penh

phone no apostrophe

phosphorous adjective
phosphorus noun

photocopy not Photostat or
Xerox (trade names)

pi the ratio of the cirumference
of a circle to its diameter, as
every schoolgirl knows

picket noun (one who pickets),
not picketer; **picketed,
picketing**

piecework

pigeonhole verb or noun

pigsty plural **pigsties**

Pilates

pill, the

pillbox

Pimm's

pin or **pin number** not Pin or PIN number

pipebomb

pipeline

Pissarro, Camille (1830-1903) French impressionist painter; his son Lucien (1863-1944) was also an artist

placename

Planning Inspectorate

plaster of paris

plateau plural **plateaux**

plateglass

playbill, playgoer, playwright

playing the race card an overused phrase

play-off

plc not PLC

P&O

pocketbook, pocketknife

poet laureate

pointe (ballet); **on pointe**, not on point or on pointe

Pokemon no accents

Polari a form of language used mostly by gay men and lesbians, derived in part from slang used by sailors, actors and prostitutes and popularised in the 1960s BBC radio comedy Round the Horne by the characters Julian and Sandy. Example: "Vada the dolly eke on the bona omee ajax" (Look at the gorgeous face on that nice man over there); "naff" is an example of Polari that has passed into more general use, as are "butch", "camp" and "dizzy"

police forces Metropolitan police (the Met after first mention), West Midlands police, New York police department (NYPD at second mention), etc

police ranks PC on all references to police constable (never WPC), other ranks full out and initial cap at first reference; thereafter abbreviation plus surname: Sgt Campbell, DC, Insp, Ch Insp, Det Supt, Ch Supt, Cmdr, etc (or just Mr, Ms or Mrs)

politburo

political correctness a term to be avoided on the grounds that it is, in Polly Toynbee's words, "an empty rightwing smear designed only to elevate its user"

political parties lc for word "party"; abbreviate if necessary (for example in parliamentary reporting) as C, Lab, Lib Dem (two words), SNP (Scottish National party, not "Scottish Nationalist party"), Plaid Cymru, SDLP (Social Democratic and Labour party), SF (Sinn Féin), UUP (Ulster Unionist party), DUP (Democratic Unionist party), Ukip (UK Independence party)

pop art

Pope, the but **the pontiff**; no need to give his name in full

poppadom

Portakabin TM

portland cement, portland stone

Port of London authority PLA on second mention

postcode

postgraduate

Post-it TM

postmodern, postmodernist

postmortem

Post Office cap up the organisation, but you buy stamps in a **post office** or **sub-post office**

postwar

Potters Bar no apostrophe

PoW abbreviation for prisoner of war

practice noun **practise** verb

practising homosexual do not use this grotesque expression; where it is necessary to discuss someone's sex life, for example a story about gay clergy, it is possible to use other expressions, eg the Anglican church demands celibacy from gay clergy but permits the laity to have sexually active relationships

precis singular and plural

pre-eminent

prefab, prefabricated

premier use only when constitutionally correct (eg leaders of Australian states or Canadian provinces), therefore not for Britain — do not use in headlines for British prime minister; exception: the Chinese traditionally give their head of government the title of premier, eg Premier Wen Jiabao (Mr Wen on second mention)

premiere no accent

Premiership use for English football (FA Premier League is the governing body, not the competition); in Scotland, however, it is the Premier League

premises of buildings and logic

prepositions appeal against, protest against/over/at, not "appealed the sentence", "protested the verdict", etc.
    Schoolchildren used to be told (by English teachers unduly

influenced by Latin) that it was ungrammatical to end sentences with a preposition, a fallacy satirised by Churchill's "this is the sort of English up with which I will not put" and HW Fowler's "What did you bring me that book to be read to out of for?"

pre-Raphaelite

presently means soon, not at present

president lc except in title: President Bush, but George Bush, the US president

press, the singular: the British press is a shining example to the rest of the world

Press Complaints Commission PCC on second mention

Press Gazette formerly UK Press Gazette

pressurised use pressured, put pressure on or pressed to mean apply pressure, ie not "they pressurised the Wolves defence"

prestigious having prestige: nothing wrong with this, despite what wise old subeditors used to tell us

Pret a Manger food
prêt à porter fashion

preteen

prevaricate "to speak or act falsely with intent to deceive" (Collins); often confused with **procrastinate**, to put something off

preventive not preventative

prewar

PricewaterhouseCoopers one word

prima donna plural **prima donnas**

prima facie not italicised

primary care trusts lc, eg Southwark primary care trust

primate another word for archbishop; Primate of All England: Archbishop of Canterbury; Primate of England: Archbishop of York; but "the primate" on second reference

primates higher mammals of the order Primates, essentially apes and humans

prime minister

Prince of Wales at first mention; thereafter Prince Charles or the prince

principal first in importance
principle standard of conduct

principality (Wales, Monaco) lc

prison officer not warder

private finance initiative PFI on second mention

privy council but **privy counsellor**

prizes Booker prize, Nobel prize, Whitbread prize, etc. *See awards*

probe a dental implement, not an inquiry or investigation

procrastinate to delay or defer; often confused with **prevaricate**

procurator fiscal

prodigal wasteful or extravagant, not a returned wanderer; the confusion arises from the biblical parable of the prodigal son

profile a noun, not a verb

program (computer); otherwise **programme**

prohibition lc for US prohibition

pro-life do not use to mean **anti-abortion** unless in a direct quote

propeller

prophecy noun
prophesy verb

pros and cons

protege male and female, no accents

protest against, over or about not, for example, "protest the election result" which has appeared on our front page

protester not protestor

proved/proven beware the creeping "proven", featuring (mispronounced) in every other TV ad; proven is not the normal past tense of prove, but a term in Scottish law ("not proven") and in certain English idioms, eg "proven record"

proviso plural **provisos**

Ps and Qs

publicly not publically

public-private partnership PPP on second mention

Public Record Office merged with the Historical Manuscripts Commission in 2003 to form the **National Archives**

Puffa TM; say **padded** or **quilted jacket** not "puffa jacket"

pundit self-appointed expert

purchase as a noun, perhaps, but use buy as a verb

put athletics **putt** golf

Pwllheli

pygmy plural **pygmies**, lc except for members of Equatorial African ethnic group

pyjamas

pyrrhic victory

al-Qaida Osama bin Laden's organisation; it means "the Base"

Qantas

qat not khat

QC use without comma, eg Cherie Booth QC

Qualifications and Curriculum Authority QCA after first mention

quarterdeck, quartermaster

Queen, the if it is necessary to say so, she is Her Majesty or HM, never HRH

Queen's College, Oxford its official name is The Queen's College (named in honour of Queen Philippa in 1341)

Queens' College, Cambridge

Queen's speech

queueing not queuing

quicklime, quicksand, quicksilver

quixotic

quiz a suspect is questioned, not quizzed (however tempting for headline purposes)

quizshow

Quorn TM

quotation marks
Use double quotes at the start and end of a quoted section, with single quotes for quoted words within that section. Place full points and commas inside the quotes for a complete quoted sentence; otherwise the point comes outside: "Mary said, 'Your style guide needs updating,' and I said, 'I agree.' " but: "Mary said updating the guide was 'a difficult and time-consuming task'."

When beginning a quote with a sentence fragment that is followed by a full sentence, punctuate according to the final part of the quote, eg The minister called the allegations "blatant lies. But in a position such as mine, it is only to be expected."

Headlines and standfirsts (sparingly), captions and display quotes all take single quote marks.

For parentheses in direct quotes, use square brackets

quotes

Take care with direct speech: our readers should be confident that words appearing in quotation marks accurately represent the actual words uttered by the speaker, though ums and ahems can be removed and bad grammar improved. If you aren't sure of the exact wording, use indirect speech.

Where a lot of material has been left out, start off a new quote with "He added: ... ", or signify this with an ellipsis.

Take particular care when extracting from printed material, for example a minister's resignation letter

'**Read over your compositions,** and where ever you meet with a passage which you think is particularly fine, strike it out'

Samuel Johnson

And introduce the speaker from the beginning, or after the first sentence: it is confusing and frustrating to read several sentences or even paragraphs of a quote before finding out who is saying it.

From the editor:
If a reader reads something in direct quotation marks in the Guardian he/she is entitled to believe that the reporter can vouch directly for the accuracy of the quote.

Copying quotes out of other newspapers without any form of attribution is simply bad journalism, never mind legally risky. If, where there are no libel issues, you're going to repeat quotes, then always say where they came from. It won't be much help in a legal action, but at least the reader can evaluate the reliability of the source. A quote in the Sunday Sport may, who knows, count for less than one from the Wall Street Journal.

If we're taking quotes off the radio or television it is our general policy to include an attribution. This matters less if it is a pooled interview or news conference which happens to be covered by, say, the BBC or Sky. If the quote comes from an exclusive interview on a radio or TV programme (eg, Today, Channel 4 News or Newsnight) we should always include an attribution

Qur'an holy book of Islam (not Koran); regarded as the word of God, having been dictated by the prophet Muhammad, so in the eyes of Muslims it is wrong to suggest the prophet "wrote" the Qur'an

Qureia, Ahmed Palestinian politician, popularly known as Abu Ala (which means "father of Ala" — it is not a nom de guerre)

racecourse, racehorse

racial terminology

Do not use ethnic to mean black or Asian people. In a British sense, they are an ethnic minority; in a world sense, of course, white people are an ethnic minority.

Just as in the Balkans or anywhere else, internal African peoples should, where possible, be called ethnic groups or communities rather than "tribes".

Avoid the word "immigrant", which is very offensive to many black and Asian people, not only because it is often incorrectly used to describe people who were born in Britain, but also because it has been used negatively for so many years that it carries imagery of "flooding", "swamping", "bogus", "scroungers", etc.

The words black and Asian should not be used as nouns, but adjectives: black people rather than "blacks", an Asian woman rather than "an Asian", etc.

Say African Caribbean rather than Afro-Caribbean

rack and ruin

racked with pain, not wracked

rackets not racquets, except in club titles

Rada Royal Academy of Dramatic Art; normally no need to spell out

Radio 1, Radio 2, Radio 3, Radio 4, 5 Live

radiographer takes x-rays
radiologist reads them

Radio Telifís Éireann Irish public broadcasting corporation

radius plural **radii**

raft something you float on; do not say "a raft of measures", which has rapidly become a

cliche (particularly in political
reporting)

railway, railway station not
the American English versions
railroad, train station

raincoat, rainfall, rainproof

Ramadan month of fasting for
Muslims

Range Rover no hyphen

Rangers not Glasgow Rangers

rarefy, rarefied

rateable

Rawlplug TM

Ray-Ban TM; it's OK to call
them **Ray-Bans**

R&B

re/re-
Use re- (with hyphen) when
followed by the vowels e or u
(not pronounced as "yu"): eg
re-entry, re-examine, re-urge.
   Use re (no hyphen) when
followed by the vowels a, i, o or
u (pronounced as "yu"), or any
consonant: eg rearm, rearrange,
reassemble, reiterate, reorder,
reuse, rebuild, reconsider.
   Exceptions: re-read; or where
confusion with another word

would arise: re-cover/recover,
re-form/reform, re-creation/
recreation, re-sign/resign

realpolitik lc, no italics

rear admiral Rear Admiral
Horatio Hornblower at first
mention, thereafter Adm
Hornblower

reafforestation not
reforestation

**received pronunciation
(RP)** a traditionally prestigious
accent, associated with public
schools and used by an
estimated 3% of the population
of England, also known as BBC
English, Oxford English or the
Queen's English; nothing to do
with **Standard English**, which
includes written as well as
spoken language and can be
(indeed, normally is) spoken
with a regional accent

recent avoid: if the date is
relevant, use it

Red Crescent, Red Cross

referendum
plural **referendums**

re-form to form again **reform**
to change for the better; we
should not take initiators' use of
the word at its face value,

particularly in cases where the paper believes no improvement is likely

refute use this much-abused word only when an argument is disproved; otherwise **contest, deny, rebut**

regalia plural, of royalty; "royal regalia" is tautologous

Regent's Park

regime no accent

register office not registry office

registrar general

regrettable

reinstate

religious right

reopen

repellant noun **repellent** adjective: you fight repellent insects with an insect repellant

repertoire an individual's range of skills or roles; **repertory** a selection of works that a theatre or dance company might perform

replaceable

report the Lawrence report, etc; use report on or inquiry into but not report into, ie not "a report into health problems"

reported speech
When a comment in the present tense is reported, use past tense: "She said: 'I like chocolate'" (present tense) becomes in reported speech "she said she liked chocolate" (not "she said she likes chocolate").

When a comment in the past tense is reported, use "had" (past perfect tense): "She said: 'I ate too much chocolate'" (past tense) becomes in reported speech "she said she had eaten too much chocolate" (not "she said she ate too much chocolate").

Once it has been established who is speaking, there is no need to keep attributing, so long as you stick to the past tense: "Anne said she would vote Labour. There was no alternative. It was the only truly progressive party", etc

republicans lc (except for US political party)

resistance, resistance fighters *see terrorism, terrorists*

restaurateur not restauranteur

retail price index (RPI)
normally no need to spell it out

Reuters

the Rev at first mention,
thereafter use courtesy title:
eg the Rev Joan Smith,
subsequently Ms Smith; never
say "Reverend Smith", "the
Reverend Smith" or "Rev Smith"

Revelation last book in the
New Testament: not Revelations,
a very common error; its full
name is The Revelation of St
John the Divine

reveille

rickety

**ricochet, ricocheted,
ricocheting**

riffle to flick through a book,
newspaper or magazine; often
confused with **rifle**, to search or
ransack and steal from, eg rifle
goods from a shop

**right wing, the right,
rightwinger** nouns
rightwing adjective

ringfence

rivers lc, eg river Thames,
Amazon river

riveted, riveting

roadside

rob you rob a person or a bank,
using force or the threat of
violence; but you **steal** a car
or a bag of money

Rock cap if referring to Gibraltar

rock'n'roll one word

role no accent

Rollerblade TM; say **inline
skates**

rollercoaster one word

Rolls-Royce

Romany plural **Roma**

Rorschach test psychological test based on the interpretation of inkblots

roughshod

Rovers Return, the (no apostrophe) Coronation Street's pub

Royal Academy of Arts usually known as the **Royal Academy**

Royal Air Force or **RAF**

Royal Ballet

Royal Botanic Garden (Edinburgh); **Royal Botanic Gardens** (London), also known as **Kew Gardens** or simply **Kew**

Royal College of Surgeons the college or the royal college is preferable to the RCS on subsequent mention

royal commission

Royal Courts of Justice

royal family

Royal London hospital

Royal Mail

Royal Marines marines after first mention

Royal Navy or the navy

Royal Opera, Royal Opera House

royal parks

RSPB, RSPCA do not normally need to be spelt out

Rubicon

rugby league, rugby union

Rule, Britannia!

rupee Indian currency
rupiah Indonesian currency

russian roulette

Saatchi

sacrilegious not sacreligious

Sadler's Wells

Safeway

Sainsbury's for the stores; the company's name is **J Sainsbury plc**

Saint in running text should be spelt in full: Saint John, Saint Paul. For names of towns, churches, etc, abbreviate St (no point) eg St Mirren, St Stephen's church. In French placenames a hyphen is needed, eg St-Nazaire, Ste-Suzanne, Stes-Maries-de-la-Mer

St Andrews University no apostrophe

St James Park home of Exeter City; **St James' Park** home of Newcastle United; **St James's Park** royal park in London

St John Ambulance not St John's and no need for Brigade

St Paul's Cathedral

St Thomas' hospital in London; not St Thomas's

saleable

Salonika not Thessaloniki

Salvation Army never the Sally Army

salvo plural **salvoes**

Sana'a capital of Yemen

sanatorium not sanitorium, plural **sanatoriums**

San Sebastián

San Siro stadium Milan

Sao Paulo Brazilian city, not Sao Paolo

Sats standard assessment tasks
SATs scholastic aptitude tests
(in the US, where they are
pronounced as individual letters)

Saumarez Smith, Charles
director of the National Gallery

Savile Row

scherzo plural **scherzos**

**schizophrenia,
schizophrenic** use only in a
medical context, never to mean
"in two minds", which is wrong,
as well as offensive to people
diagnosed with this illness

**schoolboy, schoolgirl,
schoolchildren,
schoolroom, schoolteacher**

schools Alfred Salter primary
school, Rotherhithe; King's
school, Macclesfield; Eton
college, etc

school years year 2, year 10,
key stage 1, etc

Schröder, Gerhard German
politician

Schwarzenegger, Arnold
Arnie acceptable in headlines

scientific measurements
Take care: "m" in scientific terms
stands for "milli" (1mW is 1,000th

of a watt), while "M" denotes
"mega" (1MW is a million watts);
in such circumstances it is wise
not to bung in another "m" when
you mean million, so write out,
for example, 10million C.
  amps A, volts V, watts W,
megawatts MW, milliwatts mW,
joules J, kilojoules kJ

scientific names No need to
italicise E coli (Escherichia coli)
etc. The first name (the genus) is
capped, the second (the species)
is lc — eg Quercus robur (oak
tree)

scientific terms Some silly
cliches you might wish to avoid:
you would find it difficult to
hesitate for a nanosecond (the
shortest measurable human
hesitation is probably about
250 million nanoseconds, or
a quarter of a second);
"astronomical sums" when
talking about large sums of
money is rather dated (the
national debt surpassed the
standard astronomical unit of
93 million [miles] 100 years ago)

ScotchTape TM; say **sticky
tape**

scotch whisky, scotch mist

Scotland
The following was written by a
Scot who works for the Guardian

and lives in London. Letters expressing similar sentiments come from across Britain (and, indeed, from around the world):

We don't carry much coverage of events in Scotland and to be honest, even as an expat, that suits me fine. But I do care very much that we acknowledge that Scotland is a separate nation and in many ways a separate country. It has different laws, education system (primary, higher and further), local government, national government, sport, school terms, weather, property market and selling system, bank holidays, right to roam, banks and money, churches, etc.

If we really want to be a national newspaper then we need to consider whether our stories apply only to England (and Wales) or Britain, or Scotland only. When we write about teachers' pay deals, we should point out that we mean teachers in England and Wales; Scottish teachers have separate pay and management structures and union. When we write about it being half term, we should remember that there's no such thing in Scotland. When we write about bank holiday sunshine/rain, we should remember that in Scotland the weather was probably different and it possibly wasn't even a bank holiday.

When we write a back-page special on why the English cricket team is crap, we should be careful not to refer to it as "we" and "us". When the Scottish Cup final is played, we should perhaps consider devoting more than a few paragraphs at the foot of a page to Rangers winning their 100th major trophy (if it had been Manchester United we'd have had pages and pages with Bobby Charlton's all-time fantasy first XI and a dissertation on why English clubs are the best in Europe).

These daily oversights come across to a Scot as arrogance. They also undermine confidence in what the paper is telling the reader

Scotland Office not Scottish Office

Scott, Sir George Gilbert (1811-78) architect who designed the Albert Memorial and Midland Grand Hotel at St Pancras station in London

Scott, Sir Giles Gilbert (1880-1960), grandson of the above, responsible for red telephone boxes, Bankside power station (now Tate Modern), Waterloo bridge and the Anglican cathedral in Liverpool

Scottish Enterprise

Scottish parliament
members are **MSPs**

scottish terrier not scotch;
once known as Aberdeen terrier

scouse, scouser

**seacoast, seaplane,
seaport, seashore,
seaside, seaweed**

**sea change, sea level, sea
serpent, sea sickness**

Séamus, Seán note accents in
Irish Gaelic; sean without a fada
means old

seas, oceans uc, eg Black
Sea, Caspian Sea, Pacific Ocean

seasons spring, summer,
autumn, winter, all lc

section 28

seize not sieze

**self-control, self-defence,
self-esteem, self-respect**

Sellotape TM; say **sticky
tape**

semicolon The following
sentence, from a column by
David McKie, illustrates perfectly

how to use the semicolon:
"Some reporters were brilliant;
others were less so"

senior abbreviate to **Sr** not Sen
or Snr, eg George Bush Sr

September 11
(**9/11** is acceptable)
The official death toll (revised
January 2004) of the victims of
the Islamist terrorists who
hijacked four aircraft on
September 11 2001 is 2,973.
The figure includes aircraft
passengers and crews, but not
the 19 hijackers. Of this total,
2,749 died in the attacks on the
twin towers of the World Trade
Centre (1,541 have been
identified from remains at Ground
Zero), 184 were killed in the
attack on the Pentagon, and 40
died when their plane crashed
into a field near Shanksville,
Pennsylvania.

The hijackers were: Fayez
Ahmed, Mohamed Atta, Ahmed
al-Ghamdi, Hamza al-Ghamdi,
Saeed al-Ghamdi, Hani Hanjour,
Nawaf al-Hazmi, Salem al-Hazmi,
Ahmed al-Haznawi, Khalid al-
Mihdhar, Majed Moqed, Ahmed
al-Nami, Abdulaziz al-Omari,
Marwan al-Shehhi, Mohannad
al-Shehri, Wael al-Shehri, Waleed
al-Shehri, Satam al-Suqami and
Ziad Jarrah (though dozens of
permutations of their names have
appeared in the paper, we follow

Reuters style, as for most Arabic transliterations)

Serb noun **Serbian** adjective: the Serbs ousted the Serbian dictator Slobodan Milosevic

sergeant major Sergeant Major John Ardill, subsequently Sgt Maj (not RSM or CSM) Ardill

Serious Fraud Office SFO on second mention

serjeant at arms

services, the armed forces

Sex and the City not Sex in the City

sexing up
From the editor:
Guardian readers would rather we did give them the unvarnished truth — or our best stab at it. It seems obvious enough. But inside many journalists — this goes for desk editors as much as reporters — there is a little demon prompting us to make the story as strong and interesting as possible, if not more so. We drop a few excitable adjectives around the place. We overegg. We may even sex it up.

Strong stories are good. So are interesting stories. But straight, accurate stories are even better. Readers who stick with us over any length of time would far rather judge what we write by our own Richter scale of news judgments and values than feel that we're measuring ourselves against the competition. Every time we flam a story up we disappoint somebody — usually a reader who thought the Guardian was different.

We should be different. Of course we compete fiercely in the most competitive newspaper market in the world. Of course we want to sell as many copies as possible. We've all experienced peer pressure to write something as strongly as possible, if not more so. But our Scott Trust ownership relieves us of the necessity to drive remorselessly for circulation to the exclusion of all else. In other words, we don't need to sex things up, and we shouldn't

sexuality
From a reader:
"Can I suggest your style guide should state that homosexual, gay, bisexual and heterosexual are primarily adjectives and that use of them as nouns should be avoided. It seems to me that this is both grammatically and politically preferable (politically because using them as nouns

really does seem to define people by their sexuality). I would like to read that someone is 'homosexual', not 'a homosexual', or about 'gay people', not 'gays'. Lesbian is different as it is a noun that later began to be used adjectivally, not the other way round. As an example from Wednesday, the opening line 'Documents which showed that Lord Byron … was a bisexual' rather than 'was bisexual' sounds both Daily Mail-esque and stylistically poor"

shakeout, shakeup

Shakespearean

Shankill Road Belfast

shareholder

sharia law

sheepdog

sheikh

Shepherd Market Mayfair **Shepherd's Bush** west London

Shetland or the **Shetland Isles** but never "the Shetlands"

Shia, Sunni two branches of Islam (note: not Shi'ite); plural **Shia Muslims** and **Sunni Muslims**, though Shias and Sunnis are fine if you are pushed for space

'If a writer needs a dictionary he should not write. He should have read the dictionary at least three times from beginning to end and then have loaned it to someone who needs it'

Ernest Hemingway

ships not feminine: it ran aground, not she ran aground

shipbuilder, shipbuilding, shipmate, shipowner, shipyard

shoo-in not shoe-in

shopkeeper

Shoreham-by-Sea not Shoreham on Sea

Short money payment to opposition parties to help them carry out their parliamentary functions, named after Ted Short, the Labour leader of the house who introduced it in 1975

Siamese twins do not use: they are **conjoined twins**

side-effects

sidestreet

siege not seige

Siena Tuscan city
sienna pigment

silicon computer chips
silicone breast implants

Singaporean names in three parts, eg Lee Kuan Yew

Singin' in the Rain not Singing

single quotes in headlines (but sparingly), standfirsts and captions

sink past tense **sank**, past participle **sunk**: he sinks, he sank, he has sunk

Sinn Féin

siphon not syphon

ski, skis, skier, skied, skiing

skipper usually only of a trawler

smallholding

Smith & Wesson

Smithsonian Institution not Institute

snowplough

socialism, socialist lc unless name of a party, eg Socialist Workers party

social security benefits all lc, income support, working tax credit, etc

sod's law

Sofía queen of Spain

soi-disant means self-styled, not so-called

soiree

Sotheby's

soundbite

sources Guardian journalists should use anonymous sources sparingly. We should — except in exceptional circumstances — avoid anonymous pejorative quotes. We should avoid misrepresenting the nature and number of sources, and we should do our best to give readers some clue as to the authority with which they speak. We should never, ever, betray a source. *See appendix 2: the editor's guidelines on the identification of sources*

South Bank

south south London, southwest England, the south-east, etc

southern hemisphere

south pole

Southport Visiter a newspaper, not to be confused with the **Visitor**, Morecambe

spaghetti western

Spanish names and accents
Be aware that the surname is normally the second last name, not the last, which is the mother's maiden name, eg the writer Federico García Lorca — known as García in Spain rather than Lorca — should be García Lorca on second mention. Note also that the female name Consuelo ends with an "o" not an "a".

A guide to accents follows. If in doubt do an internet search (try the word with and without an accent) and look for reputable Spanish language sites, eg big newspapers:

Surnames ending -ez take an accent over the penultimate vowel, eg Benítez, Fernández, Giménez, Gómez, González, Gutiérrez, Hernández, Jiménez, López, Márquez, Martínez, Núñez, Ordóñez, Pérez, Quiñónez, Ramírez, Rodríguez, Sáez, Vásquez, Vázquez, Velázquez. Exception: Alvarez; note also that names ending -es do not take the accent, eg Martines, Rodrigues.

Other surnames Aristízabal, Beltrán, Cáceres, Calderón, Cañizares, Chevantón, Couñago, Cúper, Dalí, De la Peña, Díaz, Forlán, García, Gaudí, Miró, Muñoz, Olazábal, Pavón, Sáenz, Sáinz, Valdés, Valerón, Verón.

Forenames Adán, Alán, Andrés, César, Darío, Elías, Fabián, Ginés, Héctor, Hernán, Iñaki, Iñés, Iván, Jesús, Joaquín, José, Lucía, María, Martín, Matías, Máximo, Míchel, Raúl, Ramón, Róger, Rubén, Sebastián, Víctor.

The forenames Ana, Angel, Alfredo, Alvaro, Cristina, Diego, Domingo, Emilio, Ernesto, Federico, Fernando, Ignacio, Jorge, Juan, Julio, Luis, Marta, Mario, Miguel, Pablo and Pedro do not usually take accents

Placenames Asunción, Bogotá, Cádiz, Catalonia, Córdoba, La Coruña, Guantánamo Bay, Guipúzcoa, Jaén, Jérez, León, Medellín, Potosí, San Sebastián, Valparaíso

Sports teams, etc América, Atlético, El Barça (FC Barcelona), Bernabéu, Bolívar, Cerro Porteño, Deportivo La Coruña, Huracán, Málaga, Peñarol

Note: Spanish is an official language in Argentina, Bolivia, Chile, Colombia, Costa Rica, Cuba, Dominican Republic, Ecuador, El Salvador, Equatorial Guinea, Guatemala, Honduras, Mexico, Nicaragua, Panama, Paraguay, Peru, Puerto Rico, Spain, Uruguay and Venezuela

Spanish customs, Spanish practices old Fleet Street expressions to be avoided

span of years 1995-99, not 1995/9, but between 1995 and 1999, not between 1995-99

spare-part surgery avoid this term

spastic do not use

Speaker, the (Commons) but **deputy speaker** (of whom there are several)

special usually redundant

Special Immigration Appeals Commission Siac or "the commission" on second mention

spelled/spelt she spelled it out for him: "the word is spelt like this"

Spice Girls Victoria Beckham was Posh Spice; Melanie Brown was Scary Spice; Emma Bunton was Baby Spice; Melanie Chisholm was Sporty Spice; Geri Halliwell was Ginger Spice

spicy not spicey

Spider-Man

spiral prices (and other things) can spiral down as well as up; try a less cliched word that doesn't suggest a circular movement

split infinitives

"The English-speaking world may be divided into (1) those who neither know nor care what a split infinitive is; (2) those who do not know, but care very much; (3) those who know and condemn; (4) those who know and distinguish. Those who neither know nor care are the vast majority, and are happy folk, to be envied."
HW Fowler, Modern English Usage, 1926

It is perfectly acceptable to sensibly split infinitives, and stubbornly to resist doing so can sound awkward and make for ambiguity: "the workers are declared strongly to favour a strike" raises the question of whether the declaration, or the favouring, is strong.

George Bernard Shaw got it about right after an editor tinkered with his infinitives: "I don't care if he is made to go quickly, or to quickly go — but go he must!"

spoiled/spoilt she spoiled her son: in fact he was a spoilt brat

spokesman, spokeswoman are preferable to "spokesperson",

but if possible attribute a quote to the organisation, eg "The AA said ... "

sponsorship

Try to avoid: we are under no obligation to carry sponsors' names. So London Marathon, not Flora London Marathon, etc. When a competition is named after a sponsor, it is unavoidable: Nationwide League, AXA League

spoonful plural **spoonfuls**

square brackets use for interpolated words in quotations, eg Mr Howard said: "Iain [Duncan Smith] has my full support"

square metres not the same as metres squared: eg 300 metres squared is 90,000 sq metres which is very different to 300 sq metres; we often get this wrong

squaw offensive, do not use

stadium plural **stadiums**

stalactites cling to the ceiling **stalagmites** grow from the ground

stalemate do not use to mean deadlock or impasse; a stalemate is the end of the game, and cannot be broken or resolved

stamp not stomp

state of the union address (US)

stationary not moving
stationery writing materials

steadfast

steamboat, steamhammer, steamship

steam engine

sten gun

step change avoid; **change** is usually adequate

stepfather, stepmother

sterling (the pound)

sticky-back plastic

stiletto plural **stilettos**

still life plural **still lifes**

stilton cheese

stimulus plural **stimuli**

stock in trade

stock market, stock exchange

storey plural **storeys** (buildings)

straightforward

straitjacket

strait-laced

strait of Dover, strait of Hormuz, etc

Strategic Rail Authority SRA on second mention

stratum plural **strata**

Street-Porter, Janet

streetwise

stretchered off do not use; say carried off on a stretcher

strippergram

stumbling block

stylebook but **style guide**

subcommittee, subcontinent, subeditor, sublet, sublieutenant, subplot, subsection

subjunctive
The author Somerset Maugham noted more than 50 years ago: "The subjunctive mood is in its death throes, and the best thing to do is put it out of its misery as soon as possible." Would that that were so. Most commonly, it is a third person singular form of

the verb expressing hypothesis, typically something demanded, proposed, imagined: he demanded that she resign at once, I propose that she be sacked, she insisted Jane sit down. The subjunctive is particularly common in American English and in formal or poetic contexts: if I were a rich man, etc. It can sound hyper-correct or pretentious, so use common sense; Fowler notes that is is "seldom obligatory"

submachine gun

submarines are boats, not ships

subpoena, subpoenaed

suchlike

suicide
Guardian journalists should exercise particular care in reporting suicide or issues involving suicide, bearing in mind the risk of encouraging others. This applies to presentation, including the use of pictures, and to describing the method of suicide. Any substances should be referred to in general rather than specific terms. When appropriate a helpline number (eg the Samaritans) should be given. The feelings of relatives should also be carefully considered

Super Bowl

supermarkets Marks & Spencer or M&S, Morrisons, Safeway, Sainsbury's, Tesco (no wonder people get confused about apostrophes)

supermodel every new face who makes a name for herself these days is labelled a supermodel; **model** is sufficient

supersede not supercede

supply, supply days (parliament)

Sure Start

surge prefer rise or increase, if that is the meaning; but surge is preferable to "upsurge"

surrealism

swap not swop

swath, swaths broad strip, eg cut a wide swath
swathe, swathes baby clothes, bandage, wrappings

swearwords
We are more liberal than any other newspaper, using words such as cunt and fuck that most of our competitors would not use.

The editor's guidelines:
First, remember the reader, and
respect demands that we should
not casually use words that are
likely to offend.

Second, use such words only
when absolutely necessary to the
facts of a piece, or to portray a
character in an article; there is
almost never a case in which we
need to use a swearword outside
direct quotes.

Third, the stronger the
swearword, the harder we ought
to think about using it.

Finally, never use asterisks,
which are just a copout

swingeing

synopsis plural **synopses**

syntax beware of ambiguous or
incongruous sentence structure:
"a man was charged with
exposing himself in court
yesterday"

**synthesis, synthesise,
synthesiser**

tableau plural **tableaux**

table d'hote

tactics singular and plural

Taiwanese names like Hong Kong and Korean names, these are in two parts with a hyphen, eg Lee Teng-hui

Tajikistan adjective **Tajik**

~~**takeoff**~~ noun **take off** verb

takeover

Takeover Panel

Taliban plural (means "students of Islamic knowledge")

talkshow

talk to not talk with

tam o'shanter woollen cap

Tampax TM; say **tampon**

T&G the Transport and General Workers' Union rebranded

Tangier not Tangiers

Tannoy TM

taoiseach Irish prime minister (prime minister is also acceptable)

~~**targeted, targeting**~~

tariff

tarot cards

taskforce

Tate
The original London gallery in Millbank, now known as **Tate Britain**, houses British art from the 16th century; **Tate Modern**, at Southwark, south London, **Tate Liverpool** and **Tate St Ives**, in Cornwall, all house modern art

tax avoidance is legal
tax evasion is illegal

taxi, taxiing of aircraft

Tbilisi capital of Georgia

teabag, teacup, teapot, teaspoon

team-mate

teams
Sports teams take plural verbs:
Australia won by an innings,
Wednesday were relegated
again, etc; but note that in a
business context they are
singular like other companies,
eg Leeds United posted its
biggest loss to date

teargas

Teasmade TM; say **teamaker**

Technicolor TM

Teesside

teetotaller

Teflon TM; say **non-stick pan**

telephone numbers
hyphenate after three or four-
figure area codes, but not five-
figure area codes: 020-7278
2332, 0161-832 7200; 01892
456789, 01227 123456; treat
mobile phone numbers as having
five-figure area codes: 07911
654321

Teletubbies they are: **Tinky
Winky** (purple), **Laa-Laa**
(yellow), **Dipsy** (green), and **Po**
(red)

television shows chatshow,
gameshow, quizshow, talkshow

temazepam

temperatures thus: 30C (85F)
— ie celsius, with fahrenheit in
brackets on first mention; but be
extremely wary (or don't bother)
converting temperature changes,
eg an average temperature
change of 2C was wrongly
converted to 36F in an article
about a heatwave (although a
temperature of 2C is about the
same as 36F, a temperature
change of 2C corresponds to a
change of about 4F)

Ten Commandments

tendinitis not tendonitis

Tenerife

tenses
We've Only Just **Begun** was playing on the radio. He **began** to **drink**; in fact he **drank** so much, he was **drunk** In no time at all. He **sank** into depression, knowing that all his hopes had been **sunk**. Finally, he **sneaked** away. Or perhaps **snuok** away (according to Pinker, the most recent irregular verb to enter the language).
See burned, dreamed, learned, spelled, spoiled

terrace houses not terraced

Terrence Higgins Trust

terrorism, terrorists
A terrorist act is directed against victims chosen either randomly or as symbols of what is being opposed (eg workers in the World Trade Centre, tourists in Bali, Spanish commuters). It is designed to create a state of terror in the minds of a particular group of people or the public as a whole for political or social ends. Although most terrorist acts are violent, you can be a terrorist without being overtly violent (eg poisoning a water supply or gassing people on the underground).
Does having a good cause make a difference? The UN says no: "Criminal acts calculated to provoke a state of terror in the general public are in any circumstances unjustifiable, whatever the considerations of a political, philosophical, ideological, racial, ethnic, religious or other nature that may be invoked to justify them."
Whatever one's political sympathies, Palestinian suicide bombers, al-Qaida, most paramilitary groups in Northern Ireland, and Eta can all reasonably be regarded as terrorists (or at least groups some of whose members perpetrate terrorist acts).
This doesn't mean that we don't have to be very careful about using the term: it is still a subjective judgment (one person's terrorist may be another person's freedom fighter). Often, alternatives such as militants, radicals, separatists, etc, may be more appropriate and less controversial, but this is a difficult area: references to the "resistance", for example, imply more sympathy to a cause than calling such fighters "insurgents". The most important thing is that, in news reporting, we are not seen — because of the language we use — to be taking sides

Tesco not Tesco's

Tessa tax-exempt special savings account, replaced by Isas

Test (cricket) the third Test, etc

Texan a person; the adjective is **Texas**: Texas Ranger, Texas oilwells, Texas tea, etc

textbook

that do not use automatically after the word "said", but it can be useful: you tend to read a sentence such as "he said nothing by way of an explanation would be forthcoming" as "he said nothing by way of an explanation" and then realise that it does not say that at all; "he said that nothing by way of an explanation would be forthcoming" is much clearer

'It will be proved to thy face that thou hast men about thee that usually talk of a noun and a verb, and such abominable words as no Christian ear can endure to hear'

Shakespeare Henry VI Part 2

that or which? that defines, which informs: this is the house that Jack built, but this house, which Jack built, is now falling down

the
Leaving "the" out often reads like jargon: say the conference agreed to do something, not "conference agreed"; the government has to do, not "government has to"; the Super League (rugby), not "Super League".

Avoid the "chancellor Gordon Brown" syndrome: do not use constructions such as "chancellor Gordon Brown said". Prominent figures can just be named, with their function at second mention: "Gordon Brown said last night" (first mention); "the chancellor said" (subsequent mentions). Where it is thought necessary to explain who someone is, write "Neil Warnock, the Sheffield United manager, said" or "the Sheffield United manager, Neil Warnock, said". In such cases the commas around the name indicate there is only one person in the position, so write "the Tory leader, Michael Howard, said" (only one person in the job), but "the former Tory prime minister John Major said" (there have been many).

lc for newspapers (the Guardian), magazines (the New Statesman), pubs (the Coach and Horses), bands (the Beatles, the Black Eyed Peas, the The), sports grounds (the Oval); uc for books (The Lord of the Rings), films (The Matrix), poems (The Waste Land), television shows (The West Wing), and placenames (The Hague)

theatregoer

theirs no apostrophe

thermonuclear

Thermos TM; say **vacuum flask**

thinktank one word

Third Reich

third way

third world lc, but **developing countries** is preferable

thoroughbred, thoroughgoing

threefold, threescore

three-line whip

thunderstorm

Tiananmen Square Beijing

Tianjin not Tientsin

tidal wave just what it says it is; **tsunami** huge wave caused by an underwater earthquake

tidewater

tikka masala

times 1am, 6.30pm, etc; 10 o'clock last night but 10pm yesterday; half past two, a quarter to three, etc; for 24-hour clock, 00.47, 23.59

tinfoil

titbit not tidbit

titles
Do not italicise or put in quotes titles of books, films, TV programmes, paintings, songs, albums or anything else. Words in titles take initial caps except for a, and, for, from, in, of, the, to (except in initial position): A Tale of Two Cities, Happy End of the World, Shakespeare in Love, The God of Small Things, War and Peace, Who Wants to Be a Millionaire?, etc. Exception: the Review. *See italics*

T-junction

to-do as in "what a to-do!"

Tolkien, JRR (1892-1973) British author and philologist, notable for writing The Lord of the Rings and not spelling his name "Tolkein"

tomato plural **tomatoes**

tonne not ton: the metric tonne is 1,000kg (2,204.62lb), the British ton is 2,240lb, and the US ton is 2,000lb; usually there is no need to convert

top 10, top 40, etc

top hat

tornado plural **tornadoes** (storm) **Tornado** plural **Tornados** (aircraft)

tortuous a tortuous road — one that winds or twists; **torturous** a torturous experience — one that involves pain or suffering

Tory party

totalisator, the tote

totalled

touchdown

Toussaint, Allen US blues musician

Toussaint, Jean US jazz musician

Toussaint L'Ouverture, Pierre Dominique (1743-1803) leader of Haiti's slave revolt of 1791 and subsequent fight for independence, which was granted in 1801

town councillor, town hall

Townshend, Pete member of the Who who didn't die before he got old

trademarks (TM) Take care: use a generic alternative unless there is a very good reason not to, eg ballpoint pen, not biro (unless it really is a Biro, in which case it takes a cap B); say photocopy rather than Xerox, etc

trade union, trade unionist, trades union council, Trades Union Congress (TUC)

tragic use with care, especially avoiding cliches such as "tragic accident"

transatlantic

Transport for London TfL on second mention

Trans-Siberian railway

Travellers uc: they are recognised as an ethnic group under the Race Relations Act

Treasury, the

treaties lc, eg Geneva convention, treaty of Nice

Trekkers how to refer to Star Trek fans unless you want to make fun of them, in which case they are **Trekkies**

trenchcoat

tricolour French and Irish

trip-hop

Trips trade-related intellectual property rights

trooper soldier in a cavalry regiment **trouper** member of a troupe, or dependable worker

trooping the colour

tropic of cancer, tropic of capricorn

the Troubles (Northern Ireland)

try to never "try and", eg "I will try to do something about this misuse of language"

tsar not czar

tsetse fly

T-shirt not tee-shirt

tsunami wave caused by an undersea earthquake; not a tidal wave

tube, the lc (London Underground is the name of the company); individual lines thus: Jubilee line, Northern line, etc; the underground

TUC Trades Union Congress, so TUC Congress is tautological; the reference should be to the TUC conference

turgid does not mean apathetic or sluggish — that's **torpid** — but swollen, congested, or (when used of language) pompous or bombastic

turkish delight

Turkmenistan adjective **Turkmen**; its citizens are Turkmen, singular **Turkman**. **Turkomans** (singular noun and adjective is **Turkoman**) are a formerly nomadic central Asian people who now form a minority in Iraq; they speak **Turkmen**

turnover noun **turn over** verb

21st century

twofold

tying

Uighur, Uighurs the Uighur people, particularly of the Xinjiang region in China

Ukraine no "the"; adjective **Ukrainian**

Ulster acceptable in headlines to mean Northern Ireland, which in fact comprises six of the nine counties of the province of Ulster

Uluru formerly known as Ayers Rock, though Ayers Rock can be used in headlines

Umist University of Manchester Institute of Science and Technology, due to merge with the University of Manchester

umlaut
In German placenames, ae, oe and ue should almost always be rendered ä, ö, ü. Family names, however, for the most part became petrified many years ago and there is no way of working out whether the e form or the

umlaut should be used; you just have to find out for each individual

UN no need to spell out United Nations, even at first mention

Unesco United Nations Educational, Scientific and Cultural Organisation; no need to spell it out

UN general assembly

UNHCR United Nations high commissioner for refugees; not commission (although the name stands for both the high commissioner and the refugee agency she/he fronts)

Unicef United Nations Children's Fund; no need to spell it out

UN secretary general

UN security council

UN world food programme

unbiased, unchristian, uncooperative

underage

underestimate, understate take care that you don't mean **overestimate** or **overstate** (we often get this wrong)

underground, the but **London Underground** for name of company

under way not underway

uninterested means not taking an interest; not synonymous with **disinterested**, which means unbiased, objective

union flag not union jack

unionists (Northern Ireland), lc except in the name of a party, eg Ulster Unionist party

United Kingdom England, Wales, Scotland and Northern Ireland; no need to write in full, say Britain or the UK

universities cap up, eg Sheffield University, Johns Hopkins University, Free University of Berlin

University College London no comma; UCL after first mention

Unknown Soldier tomb of the

unmistakable

upmarket

up to date but in an up-to-date fashion

US for United States, not USA; no need to spell out, even at first mention; America is also acceptable

utopian

U-turn

Uzbekistan adjective **Uzbek**

v (roman) for versus, not vs: England v Australia, Rushden & Diamonds v Sheffield Wednesday, etc

V&A abbreviation for Victoria and Albert Museum

Val d'Isère

Valparaíso

Valuation Office Agency VOA after first mention

Vanessa-Mae

Vanuatu formerly New Hebrides

Vargas Llosa, Mario Peruvian writer and politician

Vaseline TM

VAT value added tax; no need to spell it out

VE Day May 8 1945 **VJ Day** August 15 1945

Vehicle Inspectorate

Velázquez, Diego (1599-1660) Spanish painter

Velcro TM

veld not veldt

venal open to bribery
venial easily forgiven

venetian blind

veranda not verandah

'**Everyone has always regarded** any usage but his own as either barbarous or pedantic'

Evelyn Waugh

verdicts recorded by coroners; returned by inquest juries

vermilion

very usually very redundant

veterinary

veto, vetoes, vetoed, vetoing

vicar a cleric of the Anglican church (which also has rectors and curates, etc), not of any other denomination

vice-chairman, vice-president

vichyssoise

vie, vying

Villa-Lobos, Heitor (1887-1959) Brazilian composer

virtuoso plural **virtuosos**

vis-a-vis

vocal cords not chords

voiceover

volcano plural **volcanos**

vortex plural **vortexes**

wagon

wah-wah pedal

Wales Office not Welsh Office

walking stick

Wall's ice-cream, sausages

Wal-Mart

Wap (wireless application protocol) phones

wars do not say "before/after the war" when you mean the second world war
first world war, second world war
Gulf war (1991), **Iraq war** (2003)
Crimean, Boer, Korean, Vietnam wars
hundred years war
War of Jenkins' Ear

Was (Not Was) defunct US rock band

Waste Land, The poem by TS Eliot (not The Wasteland)

watercolour, watercourse, watermark, waterproof, waterworks

Watford Gap a service area on the M1 in Northamptonshire, named after a nearby village 80 miles north of London; nothing to do with the Hertfordshire town of Watford, with which it is sometimes confused by lazy writers who think such phrases as "anyone north of the Watford Gap" a witty way to depict the unwashed northern hordes

web, webpage, website, world wide web

weight in kilograms with imperial conversion, eg 65kg (10st 2lb)

Weight Watchers TM

welch to fail to honour an obligation, not welsh

Welch Regiment, Royal Welch Fusiliers

Welsh assembly members are AMs

welfare state

wellbeing

wellnigh

Welsh, Irvine Scottish author

welsh rarebit

west, western, the west, western Europe

western (cowboy film)

West Bank

west coast mainline

West Country

Westminster Abbey

Weyerhaeuser US pulp and paper company

wheelchair say (if relevant) that someone uses a wheelchair, not that they are "in a wheelchair" or "wheelchair-bound" — stigmatising and offensive, as well as inaccurate

whence means where from, so don't write "from whence"

whereabouts singular: her whereabouts is not known

Which? magazine

whisky plural whiskies; but **Irish** and **US whiskey**

whistleblower

white lc in racial context

white paper

Whitsuntide not Whitsun

who or whom?
From a Guardian report: "The US kept up the pressure by naming nine Yugoslav military leaders operating in Kosovo whom it said were committing war crimes." The "whom" should have been "who". That one was caught by the sub, but it is a common mistake.

If in doubt, ask yourself how the clause beginning who/whom would read in the form of a sentence giving he, him, she, her, they or them instead: if the who/whom person turns into he/she/they, then "who" is right; if it becomes him/her/them, then it should be "whom".

In the story above, "they" were allegedly committing the crimes, so it should be "who".

In this example: "Blair was attacked for criticising Howard,

whom he despised" — "whom"
is correct because he despised
"him".

But in "Blair criticised Howard,
who he thought was wrong" —
"who" is correct, because it is
"he" not "him" who is considered
wrong.

Use of "whom" has all but
disappeared from spoken
English, and seems to be going
the same way in most forms of
written English too. If you are not
sure, it is much better to use
"who" when "whom" would
traditionally have been required
than to use "whom" incorrectly
for "who", which will make you
look not just wrong but wrong
and pompous

wicketkeeper

Widdecombe, Ann Tory
minister turned Guardian agony
aunt

wide awake

Wi-Fi TM; the generic term is
**wireless computer
network**

Wimpey houses
Wimpy burgers

Windermere not Lake
Windermere; note that
Windermere is also the name of
the town

wines lc, whether taking
their name from a region (eg
beaujolais, bordeaux, burgundy,
chablis, champagne) or a grape
variety (eg cabernet sauvignon,
chardonnay, merlot, muscadet).

The regions themselves of
course are capped up: so one
might drink a burgundy from
Burgundy, or a muscadet from
the Loire valley; as are wines of
individual chateaux, eg I enjoyed
a glass of Cos d'Estournel 1970

wing commander abbreviate
on second mention to Wing Co;
Wing Commander Barry
Johnson, subsequently Wing Co
Johnson

wipeout noun **wipe out** verb

withhold

wits' end

wiz as in "she's a total wiz at
maths", not whiz or whizz

woeful

womenswear

Woolworths

working tax credit replaced
the working families tax credit

World Bank

world championship

World Cup (football, cricket, rugby)

World Health Organisation
WHO (caps) on second mention

world heritage site

World Series
It is a baseball myth that this event got its name from the New York World: originally known as the World's Championship Series, it had nothing to do with the newspaper. However, it has become tedious every time the World Series comes round to see its name cited as an example of American arrogance so please don't do it

World Trade Centre, Ground Zero but **the twin towers**

worldwide but **world wide web**

wrack seaweed
racked with guilt, not wracked
rack and ruin

WWE World Wrestling Entertainment, formerly the World Wrestling Federation

WWF the organisation that used to be known as the World Wide Fund for Nature (or, in the US, World Wildlife Fund) wishes to be known simply by its initials

xenophobe, xenophobia, xenophobic

Xerox TM; say **photocopy**

Xhosa South African ethnic group and language

Xi'an city in China where the Terracotta Warriors are located

Xmas avoid; use Christmas unless writing a headline, up against a deadline, and desperate

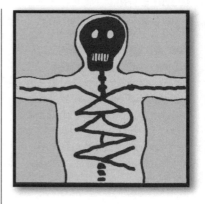

x-ray

Yahoo! (the company)

year say 2004, not "the year 2004"; for a span of years use hyphen, thus: 2004-05 not 2004/5

yearbook

Yekaterinburg

Yellow Pages TM

Yemen not "the Yemen"

yes campaign, no campaign not Yes or "yes" campaign

yo-yo

Yo-Yo Ma cellist

Yorkshire North Yorkshire, South Yorkshire, West Yorkshire but **east Yorkshire**

Yorkshire dales but **North York Moors** national park

yorkshire pudding, yorkshire terrier

Yorkshire Ripper

Young, Lady full title Lady Young of Old Scone (Labour): chair of English Nature; Lady Young of Farnworth (Tory), a former leader of the Lords and staunch defender of section 28, died in 2002

yours no apostrophe

yuan Chinese currency; we don't call it renminbi

Zapatero, José Luis Rodríguez Spanish politician; Mr Zapatero on second mention

zeitgeist

Zellweger, Renée

Zephaniah, Benjamin

zero plural **zeros**

Zeta-Jones, Catherine

zeugma "The queen takes counsel and tea" (Alexander Pope)

zhoosh an example of gay slang (*see Polari*), used in the fashion industry and on US television shows such as Will and Grace and Queer Eye for the Straight Guy, it has various shades of meaning: (noun) clothing, ornamentation; (verb) zhoosh your hair, zhoosh yourself up; **zhooshy** (adjective) showy

zigzag no hyphen

zloty Polish unit of currency

References

www.guardian.co.uk/styleguide

Amis, Kingsley: The King's English, A Guide to Modern Usage (HarperCollins, 1997)

Baker, Paul: Fantabulosa, A Dictionary of Polari and Gay Slang (Continuum, 2002)

Bauer, Laurie and Trudgill, Peter (eds): Language Myths (Penguin, 1998)

Bierce, Ambrose: The Devil's Dictionary (Neal Publishing Company, 1911; reprinted by Dover Publications, 1993)

Burchfield, RW: The New Fowler's Modern English Usage (OUP, revised 3rd edition, 1998)

Collins English Dictionary (21st century edition)

Crystal, David: The Cambridge Encyclopedia of English (Cambridge University Press, 1995)

Crystal, David: Who Cares About English Usage? (Penguin, 1984)

The Economist Style Guide (Profile Books, 1998)

Hicks, Wynford and Holmes, Tim: Subediting for Journalists (Routledge, 2002)

Inman, Colin: The Financial Times Style Guide (Pitman, 1994)

Palmer, FR: The English Verb (Longman, 2nd edition, 1987)

Quirk, R; Greenbaum, S; Leech, G; Svartvik, J: A Comprehensive Grammar of the English Language (Longman, 1985)

Pinker, Steven: The Language Instinct (Penguin, 1994)

Pinker, Steven: Words and Rules (Phoenix, 1999)

Wyner, Ruth: From the Inside (Aurum, 2003)

Appendix 1
The Guardian's editorial code

"A newspaper's primary office is the gathering of news. At the peril of its soul it must see that the supply is not tainted."

The most important currency of the Guardian is trust. This is as true today as when CP Scott marked the centenary of the founding of the paper with his famous essay on journalism in 1921 (*see appendix 3*).

The purpose of this code is, above all, to protect and foster the bond of trust between the paper and its readers, and therefore to protect the integrity of the paper and of the editorial content it carries.

By observing the code, journalists working for the Guardian will be protecting not only the paper but also the independence, standing and reputation of themselves and their colleagues. It is important that freelances working for the Guardian also abide by these guidelines while on assignment for the paper.

Press Complaints Commission code of conduct
The Guardian — in common with most other papers in Britain — considers the PCC's code of conduct to be a sound statement of ethical behaviour for journalists. It is written into our terms of employment that staff should adhere to the code of conduct.

Professional practice

Anonymous quotations
We recognise that people will often speak more honestly if they are allowed to speak anonymously. The use of non-attributed quotes can therefore often assist the reader towards a truer understanding of a subject than if a journalist confined him/herself to quoting bland on-

the-record quotes. But if used lazily or indiscriminately anonymous quotes become a menace.

We should be honest about our sources, even if we can't name them.

The New York Times policy on pejorative quotes is worth bearing in mind: "The vivid language of direct quotation confers an unfair advantage on a speaker or writer who hides behind the newspaper, and turns of phrase are valueless to a reader who cannot assess the source."

There may be exceptional circumstances when anonymous pejorative quotes may be used, but they will be rare — and only after consultation with the senior editor of the day. In the absence of specific approval we should paraphrase anonymous pejorative quotes.

Children

Special care should be taken when dealing with children (under the age of 16). Heads of departments must be informed when children have been photographed or interviewed without parental consent.

Copy approval

The general rule is that no one should be given the right to copy approval. In certain circumstances we may allow people to see copy or quotes but we are not required to alter copy. We should avoid offering copy approval as a method of securing interviews or cooperation.

Direct quotations

Should not be changed to alter their context or meaning.

Errors

It is the policy of the Guardian to correct significant errors as soon as possible. Journalists have a duty to cooperate frankly and openly with the readers' editor and to report errors to him. All complaints should be brought to the attention of a department head, the managing editor or the readers' editor. All journalists should read both the daily and weekly column.

Fairness
"The voice of opponents no less than of friends has a right to be heard … It is well be to be frank; it is even better to be fair" (CP Scott, 1921). The more serious the criticism or allegations we are reporting the greater the obligation to allow the subject the opportunity to respond.

Grief
People should be treated with sensitivity during periods of grief and trauma.

Language
Respect for the reader demands that we should not casually use words that are likely to offend. Use swearwords only when absolutely necessary to the facts of a piece, or to portray a character in an article; there is almost never a case in which we need to use a swearword outside direct quotes. The stronger the swearword, the harder we ought to think about using it. Avoid using in headlines, pull quotes and standfirst and never use asterisks, which are just a copout.

Legal
Our libel and contempt laws are complex, and constantly developing. The consequences of losing actions can be expensive and damaging for our reputation. Staff should a) familiarise themselves with the current state of the law and seek training if they feel unconfident about aspects of it; b) consult our in-house legal department or night lawyers about specific concerns on stories; c) read the regular legal bulletins about active cases and injunctions emailed by the legal department.

Payment
In general, the Guardian does not pay for stories, except from bona fide freelance sources. The editor or his deputies must approve rare exceptions.

PCC and libel judgments
Judgments by the PCC and the outcome of defamation actions relating to the Guardian should be reported promptly.

Photographs

Digitally enhanced or altered images, montages and illustrations should be clearly labelled as such.

Plagiarism

Staff must not reproduce other people's material without attribution. The source of published material obtained from another organisation should be acknowledged including quotes taken from other newspaper articles. Bylines should be carried only on material that is substantially the work of the bylined journalist. If an article contains a significant amount of agency copy then the agency should be credited.

Privacy

In keeping with both the PCC code and the Human Rights Act we believe in respecting people's privacy. We should avoid intrusions into people's privacy unless there is a clear public interest in doing so. Caution should be exercised about reporting and publishing identifying details, such as street names and numbers, that may enable others to intrude on the privacy or safety of people who have become the subject of media coverage.

Race

In general, we do not publish someone's race or ethnic background or religion unless that information is pertinent to the story. We do not report the race of criminal suspects unless their ethnic background is part of a description that seeks to identify them or is an important part of the story (for example, if the crime was a hate crime).

Sources

Sources promised confidentiality must be protected at all costs. However, where possible, the sources of information should be identified as specifically as possible.

Subterfuge

Journalists should generally identify themselves as Guardian employees when working on a story. There may be instances involving stories of exceptional public interest where this does not apply, but this needs the approval of a head of department.

Personal behaviour and conflicts of interest

The Guardian values its reputation for independence and integrity. Journalists clearly have lives, interests, hobbies, convictions and beliefs outside their work on the paper. Nothing in the following guidelines is intended to restrict any of that. It is intended to ensure that outside interests do not come into conflict with the life of the paper in a way that either compromises the Guardian's editorial integrity or falls short of the sort of transparency that our readers would expect. The code is intended to apply to all active outside interests which, should they remain undeclared and become known, would cause a fair-minded reader to question the value of a contribution to the paper by the journalist involved.

These are guidelines rather than one-size-fits-all rules. If you are employed as a columnist — with your views openly on display — you may have more latitude than a staff reporter, who would be expected to bring qualities of objectivity to their work. (The Washington Post's code has some sound advice: "Reporters should make every effort to remain in the audience, to stay off the stage, to report the news, not to make the news.") If in doubt, consult a head of department, the managing or deputy editors, or the editor himself.

Commercial products
No Guardian journalist or freelance primarily associated with the Guardian should endorse commercial products unless with the express permission of their head of department or managing editor.

Confidentiality
Desk editors with access to personal information relating to other members of staff are required to treat such information as confidential, and not disclose it to anyone except in the course of discharging formal responsibilities.

Conflicts of interest

Guardian staff journalists should avoid holding office, including directorships, whether paid or voluntary, or be otherwise actively involved in any outside organisation, company or political party where a conflict of interest exists or could arise. As a general rule staff should ensure that no outside personal, philosophical or financial interests conflict with their professional performance of duties at the Guardian, or could be perceived to do so.

Declarations of interest

1 It is always necessary to declare an interest when the journalist is writing about something with which he or she has a significant connection. This applies to both staff journalists and freelances writing for the Guardian. The declaration should be to a head of department or editor during preparation. Full transparency may mean that the declaration should appear in the paper or website as well.

2 A connection does not have to be a formal one before it is necessary to declare it. Acting in an advisory capacity in the preparation of a report for an organisation, for example, would require a declaration every time the journalist wrote an article referring to it.

3 Some connections are obvious and represent the reason why the writer has been asked to contribute to the paper. These should always be stated at the end of the writer's contribution even if he or she contributes regularly, so long as the writer is writing about his or her area of interest.

4 Generally speaking a journalist should not write about or quote a relative or partner in a piece, even if the relative or partner is an expert in the field in question. If, for any reason, an exception is made to this rule, the connection should be made clear.

5 Commissioning editors should ensure that freelances asked to write for the Guardian are aware of these rules and make any necessary declaration.

Declarations of corporate interest

The Guardian is part of a wider group of media companies. We should be careful to acknowledge that relationship in stories. Anyone writing a story concerning Guardian-related businesses should seek comments and/or confirmation in the normal way. Staff should familiarise themselves with the companies and interests we have. Details are on the Guardian Media Group website (www.gmgplc.co.uk/gmgplc/businesses/businessesintro).

Financial reporting

For many years the Guardian's City office has maintained a register of personal shares. All staff are expected to list all shares that they own, any transactions in those shares and any other investments which they believe ought to be properly disclosed because of a potential conflict of interest. While it is acceptable for financial members to own shares, it is not acceptable for them to be market traders on a regular basis. It is most important that the register is kept and that all information in it is up to date. The attention of Guardian journalists is also drawn to the provisions of the PCC code of practice and to the PCC's recently strengthened guidelines on financial journalism. These read:

1 Even where the law does not prohibit it, journalists must not use for their own profit financial information they receive in advance of its general publication, nor should they pass such information to others.

2 They must not write about shares or securities in whose performance they know that they or their close families have a significant financial interest without disclosing the interest to the editor or financial editor.

3 They must not buy or sell, directly or through nominees or agents, shares or securities about which they have written recently or about which they intend to write in the near future.

Freelance work

As a general rule avoid freelance writing for house magazines of particular businesses or causes if the contribution could be interpreted as an endorsement of the concern. If in doubt consult your head or department.

Freebies

1 Staff should not use their position to obtain private benefit for themselves or others.

2 The Guardian and its staff will not allow any payment, gift or other advantage to undermine accuracy, fairness or independence. Any attempts to induce favourable editorial treatment through the offer of gifts or favours should be reported to the editor. Where relevant the Guardian will disclose these payments, gifts or other advantages.

3 We should make it clear when an airline, hotel or other interest has borne the cost of transporting or accommodating a journalist. Acceptance of any such offer is conditional on the Guardian being free to assign and report or not report any resulting story as it sees fit.

4 Except in some areas of travel writing it should never need to be the case that the journalist's partner, family or friends are included in any free arrangement. When a partner, family member or friend accompanies the journalist on a trip, the additional costs should generally be paid for by the journalist or person accompanying the journalist.

5 Staff should not be influenced by commercial considerations — including the interests of advertisers — in the preparation of material for the paper.

6 Gifts of other than an insignificant value — say, more than £25 — should be politely returned or may be entered for the annual raffle of such items for charity, "the sleaze raffle".

Guardian connections

Staff members should not use their positions at the Guardian to seek any benefit or advantage in personal business, financial or commercial transactions not afforded to the public generally. Staff should not use Guardian stationery in connection with non-Guardian matters or cite a connection with the paper to resolve consumer grievances, get quicker service or seek discount or deals.

Outside engagements or duties

Staff should inform their immediate editor if, in their capacity as an employee of the Guardian, they intend to:

1 Give evidence to any court.

2 Chair public forums or seminars arranged by professional conference organisers or commercial organisations.

3 Undertake any outside employment likely to conflict with their professional duties at the Guardian.

4 Chair public or political forums or appear on platforms in any capacity that might give the perception of advocacy of a particular position where the journalist might reasonably be expected to be neutral.

5 Make representations or give evidence to any official body in connection with material that has been published in the Guardian.

Relationships

Staff members should not write about, photograph or make news judgments about any individual related by blood or marriage or with whom the staff member has a close personal, financial or romantic relationship. A staff member who is placed in a circumstance in which the potential for this kind of conflict exists should advise his or her department head.

Appendix 2

The editor's guidelines on the identification of sources

We should use anonymous sources sparingly. We should — except in exceptional circumstances — avoid anonymous pejorative quotes. We should avoid misrepresenting the nature and number of sources, and we should do our best to give readers some clue as to the authority with which they speak. We should never, ever, betray a source.

We all understand the reasons why. People will frequently only say interesting and important things if they can do so anonymously. Sometimes the reasons are ignoble (cowardice), sometimes noble (whistleblowing). At Westminster, in particular, what is accurate is often not on the record. So, obviously, much has to be left to the judgment of the reporter. Sometimes the sensitivity may be such that writers may even have to be economical with the truth in identifying the nature of the source. Such occasions should be rare.

Anonymous pejorative quotes may only be used after consultation with the senior editor of the day. In taking the decision whether to allow the quote the editor might consider such factors as:

Is the source a respected person who is well placed to pass judgment on the subject in question?

Does he/she have direct or indirect knowledge? Is it authoratitive?

Insofar as one can judge, what are his or her motives in a) speaking pejoratively of someone, and b) demanding anonymity?

Can a public interest case be made for including the information in direct quotes?

In the absence of specific approval we should paraphrase anonymous pejorative quotes.

In all this, Guardian journalists simply have to bear in mind the innocent reader, and the cumulative effect of ploughing through a paper in which a significant degree of information is passed on without any means of knowing how to evaluate it. We're effectively asking readers to take a lot on trust. And the one thing we know from all surveys is that readers are increasingly sceptical about placing their trust in newspapers (though, thankfully, Guardian readers place a very great degree of trust in the Guardian).

It is — obviously — preferable if you can persuade a source to go on the record. Where this is out of the question think of the poor reader and try and give him/her some help. "One source said last night" is, in most circumstances, so vague as to be meaningless. The reader cannot evaluate the worth of the quote since he/she has absolutely no clue as to who the source is or whether it knows what it is talking about.

If vagueness is the only option, is it possible to explain why, or to elaborate on the understanding between source and reporter? Better still is to press your source for some form of identification. So, it is best to be a specific as possible. "One MP", or "a government colleague" is so weak as to be meaningless. "Senior minister" is an advance. "Cabinet minister with direct knowledge of the negotiations" is better still. By now the reader can genuinely evaluate the worth of the remark.

I know you know that the most vaguely sourced story can also be the most authoritative. Just remember that the reader doesn't.

There is a similar difficulty in trying to set a rule of thumb about the number of sources we need before we'll print something. It's pretty obvious that it's generally good journalistic practice to speak to as many people as possible in putting together a story. You test the information Source A gives you against the information Source B gives you. You may even be reluctant to ring Source C in case he/she knocks down the story from Sources A and B. Ring Source C.

Equally, there are instances when a person you know to be truthful tells you something from his or her own personal knowledge. If the Archbishop of Canterbury rang to tell you he was resigning tomorrow, you'd print it.

The difficulty comes where a reliable, well-placed and knowledgeable source mixes information of which he/she has personal, first-hand knowledge, with material of which he/she has less direct knowledge.

He/she may, in other words, be a good, single source for some information, while other parts — from the same person — would require verification from another source.

Any reporter who has spent more than a morning in court learns the difference between direct evidence and hearsay evidence. One carries weight in court, the other doesn't. Journalism can seldom aspire to be as rigorous as legal proceedings. But we should bear in mind that fundamental distinction between types of information and types of source, if for no other reason than your story might end up in court.

A good general rule might be this: stories should wherever possible be multi-sourced. Where that is not possible, the reliance on a single source should be made clear to desk editors and the matter discussed fully. The desk editor may well ask about such matters as: why there is no other way of verifying the story; whether the single source is trusted and in a position to know what they are divulging to us; and whether the story is in the public interest. If there is a chance that additional sources could be obtained by holding off publication by a day or even a few days, then we may want to wait, unless there is an overwhelming need — not just the general desire for competitive edge — to get the story out immediately.

Finally, we should, as ever, guard against the lazy habit of using quotes from other papers when pressed at deadline — and we should always attribute the source of any such lifted quotes. Wherever possible we should strive to speak directly to relevant parties.

This is a counsel of perfection. We will sometimes, for any number of reasons, slip below these standards. That doesn't mean that we shouldn't aspire to them. There are individual departments and specialisms — City and intelligence matters — where sourcing is particularly difficult (see note from Paul Murphy below). But, over time, the more careful and watchful we are the more we will be trusted — by both readers and sources.

Alan Rusbridger

Attribution in business reporting

There are a number of special problems associated with attribution in business and financial reporting. A casual reader might come to the conclusion that many of the stories on the finance pages are poorly sourced, with the number of anonymous far outweighing the number of on-the-record statements.

There are clear reasons for this:

1 All publicly listed companies, their directors and advisers, are under a duty to inform the entire stock market of any potentially price sensitive news at the earliest opportunity. In practice, this means they are bound to issue formal statements to news agencies and stock market information suppliers whenever they have something to say which may affect the company's share price.

This means they cannot talk on the record about anything of substance which is not already in the public domain. In fact, the breach of this rule can be a criminal act under the legislative cocktail of Financial Services and Markets Act, Insider Dealing Act and various Companies Acts.

2 Of course, company directors and corporate financiers do talk, otherwise the business pages would be very dull indeed. But their identity has to be protected on a routine and constant basis. This means that any piece breaking a City or business story will invariably have smudged, anonymous sourcing. Since any director/adviser suspected of leaking information to the press will at the very least be reprimanded by authorities such as the stock exchange, business journalists often go to some lengths to disguise a source. Corporate financiers become industry analysts, the director of a company can simply become "an observer", etc.

3 Under certain circumstances, such as during takeover bids, flows of information in and around the City are given police state-type treatment. Regulators, from the Takeover Panel, for example, will on occasion ring journalists directly, trying to get information on who had made certain statements. In theory, journalists can be

hauled in front of Department of Trade and Industry investigations with no right to silence, and some officials at the Financial Services Authority, the City watchdog, believe they also have the right to compel financial journalists to provide information in certain circumstances. It goes without saying that the Guardian has and will continue to resist all such attempts to glean information on sources, but the fact that the threat exists underlines the sensitivities over business sourcing.

4 It is also worth noting that virtually all telephone conversations in and around the City of London are recorded on a routine basis. Sophisticated voice-reading software is used to search these tapes for leaks, etc. Also, many sources, such as stockbrokers, would be fired instantly if it emerged they were speaking to the press. There is a general paranoia in the business world over flows of information and we have little hope of demanding that the formal/informal channels of information change their procedures to suit us.

How do we deal with this? The simple answer is by making sure the stories are correct, whatever the printed description of the "source", and then trading on our reputation.

If we demand attribution, the simple response would be "OK, you can quote me saying 'no comment'," but even here there would be nervousness since the person would feel under suspicion for even being seen to pick up the phone.

It is illustrative to look at the Wall Street Journal, which uses a particularly coy description for its sources: "People familiar with the negotiations/company/deal said … "

Paul Murphy
Financial editor

Appendix 3

Centenary of the Manchester Guardian Thursday May 5 1921

A hundred years is a long time; it is a long time even in the life of a newspaper, and to look back on it is to take in not only a vast development in the thing itself, but a great slice in the life of the nation, in the progress and adjustment of the world.

In the general development the newspaper, as an institution, has played its part, and no small part, and the particular newspaper with which I personally am concerned has also played its part, it is to be hoped, not without some usefulness. I have had my share in it for a little more than fifty years; I have been its responsible editor for only a few months short of its last half-century; I remember vividly its fiftieth birthday; I now have the happiness to share in the celebration of its hundredth. I can therefore speak of it with a certain intimacy of acquaintance. I have myself been part of it and entered into its inner courts. That is perhaps a reason why, on this occasion, I should write in my own name, as in some sort a spectator, rather than in the name of the paper as a member of its working staff.

In all living things there must be a certain unity, a principle of vitality and growth. It is so with a newspaper, and the more complete and clear this unity the more vigorous and fruitful the growth. I ask myself what the paper stood for when first I knew it, what it has stood for since and stands for now. A newspaper has two sides to it. It is a business, like any other, and has to pay in the material sense in order to live. But it is much more than a business; it is an institution; it reflects and it influences the life of a whole community; it may affect even wider destinies. It is, in its way, an instrument of government. It plays on the minds and consciences of men. It may educate, stimulate, assist, or it may do the opposite. It has, therefore, a moral as well as a material existence, and its character and influence are in the main determined by the balance of these two forces. It may make profit or power its first object, or it may conceive itself as fulfilling a higher and more exacting function.

I think I may honestly say that, from the day of its foundation, there has not been much doubt as to which way the balance tipped as far as regards the conduct of the paper whose fine tradition I inherited and which I have had the honour to serve through all my working life. Had it not been so, personally, I could not have served it. Character is a subtle affair, and has many shades and sides to it. It is not a thing to be much talked about, but rather to be felt. It is the slow deposit of past actions and ideals. It is for each man his most precious possession, and so it is for that latest growth of time the newspaper. Fundamentally it implies honesty, cleanness, courage, fairness, a sense of duty to the reader and the community. A newspaper is of necessity something of a monopoly, and its first duty is to shun the temptations of monopoly. Its primary office is the gathering of news. At the peril of its soul it must see that the supply is not tainted. Neither in what it gives, nor in what it does not give, nor in the mode of presentation must the unclouded face of truth suffer wrong. Comment is free, but facts are sacred. 'Propaganda', so called, by this means is hateful. The voice of opponents no less than that of friends has a right to be heard. Comment also is justly subject to a self-imposed restraint. It is well to be frank; it is even better to be fair. This is an ideal. Achievement in such matters is hardly given to man. We can but try, ask pardon for shortcomings, and there leave the matter.

But, granted a sufficiency of grace, to what further conquests may we look, what purpose serve, what task envisage? It is a large question, and cannot be fully answered. We are faced with a new and enormous power and a growing one. Whither is the young giant tending? What gifts does he bring? How will he exercise his privilege and powers? What influence will he exercise on the minds of men and on our public life? It cannot be pretended that an assured and entirely satisfactory answer can be given to such questions. Experience is in some respects disquieting. The development has not been all in the direction which we should most desire.

One of the virtues, perhaps almost the chief virtue, of a newspaper is its independence. Whatever its position or character, at least it should have a soul of its own. But the tendency of newspapers, as of other businesses, in these days is towards amalgamation. In proportion, as the function of a newspaper has developed and its organisation expanded, so have its costs increased. The smaller newspapers have had a hard struggle; many of them have disappeared. In their place we have great organisations controlling a whole series of publications of various kinds and even of differing or opposing politics. The process may be inevitable, but clearly there are drawbacks. As organisation grows personality may tend to disappear. It is much to control one newspaper well, it is perhaps beyond the reach of any man, or any body of men, to control half a dozen with equal success. It is possible to exaggerate the danger, for the public is not undiscerning. It recognises the authentic voices of conscience and conviction when it finds them, and it has a shrewd intuition of what to accept and what to discount.

This is a matter which in the end must settle itself, and those who cherish the older ideal of a newspaper need not be dismayed. They have only to make their papers good enough in order to win, as well as to merit, success, and the resources of a newspaper are not wholly measured in pounds, shillings, and pence. Of course the thing can only be done by competence all round, and by that spirit of co-operation right through the working staff that only a common ideal can inspire.

There are people who think you can run a newspaper about as easily as you can poke a fire, and that knowledge, training, and aptitude are superfluous endowments. There have even been experiments on this assumption, and they have not met with success. There must be competence, to start with, on the business side, just as there must be in any large undertaking, but it is a mistake to suppose that the business side of a paper should dominate, as sometimes happens, not without distressing consequences.

A newspaper, to be of value, should be a unity, and every part of it should equally understand and respond to the purposes and ideals which animate it. Between its two sides there should be a happy marriage, and editor and business manager should march hand in hand, the first, be it well understood, just an inch or two in advance. Of the staff much the same thing may be said. They should be a friendly company. They need not, of course, agree on every point, but they should share in the general purpose and inheritance. A paper is built up upon their common and successive labours, and their work should never be task work, never merely dictated. They should be like a racing boat's crew, pulling well together, each man doing his best because he likes it, and with a common and glorious goal.

That is the path of self-respect and pleasure; it is also the path of success. And what a work it is! How multiform, how responsive to every need and every incident of life! What illimitable possibilities of achievement and of excellence! People talk of 'journalese' as though a journalist were of necessity a pretentious and sloppy writer; he may be, on the contrary, and very often is, one of the best in the world. At least he should not be content to be much less. And then the developments. Every year, almost every day, may see growth and fresh accomplishments, and with a paper that is really alive, it not only may, but does. Let anyone take a file of this paper, or for that matter any one of half a dozen other papers, and compare its whole make-up and leading features today with what they were five years ago, ten years ago, twenty years ago, and he will realise how large has been the growth, how considerable the achievement. And this is what makes the work of a newspaper worthy and interesting. It has so many sides, it touches life at so many points, at every one there is such possibility on improvement and excellence. To the man, whatever his place on the paper, whether on the editorial or business, or even what may be regarded as the mechanical side — this also vitally important in its place — nothing should satisfy short of the best, and the best must always seem a little ahead of the actual. It is here that ability counts and that character counts, and it is on these that a newspaper, like every great undertaking, if it is to be worthy of its power and duty, must rely.

CP Scott
Editor